"GI QUEEN"

"GI QUEEN"

By

Robin Natrigo

1stBooks – rev. 5/3/00

ABOUT THE BOOK

GI Queen is a part fact, part fiction account of my experience in a unit of the army based at Ft. Bragg, N.C.

My friend from that military experience who has lived nearby after our discharge, related to me some of the experiences he and his group of friends at Ft. Bragg encountered. I added some of my own experiences and included times we went together on our after hours escapades.

Robin and Rick were in the army together, in the same company and the same astrological sign, both being aries. They were born a few days apart. Rick was a blonde on the order of Doris Day, whose birthday he shared. Robin on the other side of the coin was brunette and on the unbubbly side. Rick couldn't stand the mention of Doris Day. He was flamboyant and outgoing and quite an exhibitionist. Whenever he espied a romantic interest, he went after them rather shamelessly. This is how the two had met. Robin had been riding in the ambulance with the members of the medical unit, who were his friends. They had just taken a troop to the fort hospital. Robin attended to the patient, who had an asthma attack. Robin often helped out whenever he was available and the medical unit didn't hesitate to ask. The driver of the ambulance had been a guy named Shannon, who happened to be well muscled and Irish good looking. Rick bounced his bountiful buttocks up and down, calling out "Shannon! Shannon!" This occurred as the ambulance pulled up to the Reception Station. Robin caught his first glimpse of a California blonde in action. Robin had no idea that whomever this person happened to be or that he was from California, but Rick never let him forget it afterwards. They instantly became fast friends on post and spent most of their free time together. Rick of course approached Robin wanting to know who Shannon was and absolutely nothing else. The men on post were drawn to these two with their contrasting good looks. Robin and Rick would often spend their Saturdays together scouting out old abandoned houses. This of course, was Rick's idea. Rick was mad about antiques. One such day Rick spied a house that truly looked as if possessed possibilities. Rick was thinking of encountering hordes of treasure. He sent all of this collection regularly home by freight. His mother received all of this booty to be stored in

1

a garage that Rick had rented. When they opened the door Rick's face lit up the the dark house. He truly looked like a ray of sunshine as they trudged in. Robin of course followed, not quite sharing Rick's interest in old things. The pair opened the door and got through the cobwebs and debri. They found the stairs and Robin watched as Rick's buttocks jellied up the stairs. Rick had on the tightest levi strauss blue cords, which were very much in vogue at the time. Once the pair reached the upstairs area Rick located an old trunk. He envisioned this as a pirate's chest, which he later painted black and gold. Robin couldn't believe what a little beaver Rick was. The two of them would often go roller skating in town at a place called Skatetown. They would also skate at the USO rink and attend a buffet there on Sundays. The buffet was compliments of the local Fayetteville women's society. Robin and Rick loved roller skating especially to their favorite songs.

The two would bounce along Fayetteville's sidewalks singing various tunes of that era. The bus containing the troops going or coming from town would pass them and there would always be a whistle or a yell. They promoted a lot of wolf calls during their time there. Rick got involved with a local teenager named Ken. They would see each other at the varios things and places Rick frequented. One of these places was the roller rink which Rick loved. Ken would often skate by and place a pinch of Rick's behind, which delighted Rick. They would often skate together side by side. No one was aware of their relationship and they could have cared less, if they were. Robin would watch as Rick carried on shamelessly with this teenager. This reminded Robin of a May December affair or Mrs Robinson and Benjamin. Ken was all of sixteen and Rick was twentythree. He was goodlooking and strongly built

2

and that was all that Rick cared about. Ken had a job at the theater on Fayetteville's main drag. This was a Vegas style boulevard, called oddly enough, Hay street.

Robin and Rick would also go to the YMCA dances pretending to be local teens. They passed easily and had a ball. There were sock hops on the skating floor at skate town and they went to these. Rick would meet his teen friend Ken at the theatre in town where he worked They would often go to Ken's home and talk with the boy's stepfather. He didn't at all suspect that Ken and Rick were involved romantically. Robin thought Rick's behavior was brazen compared to his own. Robin had not had his first boyfriend until he entered the army. Rick with his California ways just amazed him. He would teach Robin a lot about coming out. Robin and Rick were transexuals, in society's eyes they were males, but in every males eyes, females. The two of them entered the army thinking it was the end of the world for them, but instead a whole new world opened up for them that they didn't even know existed. Well they certainly did now. Rick and Ken carried on like lovebirds. Ken was experiencing his sexual awakening at Rick's hands. He had the standard one prior to this but this one was truly unstandard. They carried on until Rick's time on the base was up and he was to return home to California. Rick bought himself a car, he was tired of bouncing his behind on the highway to hitch a ride. Robin and Rick worked at the Reception Station on base and it was close to a town called Spring Lake, or Sprung Leak as some soldiers like to call it. Robin and Rick decided to take the car to S.C. to visit Robin's brother and his family. They took off in the old station wagon with much anticipation. They stopped off on the way to photograph each other in the cotton fields and Rick had

3

Robin take a picture of him next to an old black cotton picker. He was smiling and cooperative. The sun was glowing and Robin's blue black hair and Rick's blonde mane looked radiant to the Carolina sun. Rick had a bubbly personality like his buttocks. They had a warm greeting by Robin's family, his brother was away at the time serving another hitch in Vietnam. Robin's sister in law was from Memphis and was very hospitable. The children loved them both. They made it back after the weekend was up. They were glad to be back in the secure confines of the military. The guys were happy to have them back, they missed seeing them take their evening strolls together in their tight pants. It wasn't long before Robin introduced Rick to Demorest a very hot number. Robin and he used to apply hairspray together in the latrine before it became legal for men to wear it. Demorest was a perfect type for it with his long silky straight hair. It was a light brown with golden highlights. It was long compared to conventional military standards. The front would grace his forehead becomingly. He was striking so Rick was all exited on meeting him. The Reception Station was lax compared to the rest of the post so they all took advantage and grew their hair. Robin would touch his up in the latrine with black dye with others coming in and out. Rick came by Robin's barracks one night and called out Demorest's name rather loud and shamelessly in his high pitched voice. First it was Shannon now it was Demorest. Robin looked out of his window downstairs and Demorest looked out of his upstairs. Rick went up in pursuit of Demorest after very briefly acknowledging Robin's presence. His buttocks were really quivering up the stairs in hot pursuit. Demorest didn't share the enthusiasm that Rick had in their relationship. He was merely amused by all the attention Rick afforded him. He was rather used or familiar to been

4

made a fuss over. Robin interested him more and he thought Robin was more of a lady.

He never got around to showing his feelings toward Robin up until now. Robin was the object of many men's attention in the barracks. He used the latrine mostly at night for his showers. Sometimes he would shower over the orderly room building, it had a latrine complete with showers which no one used. The occasions when he did venture into the latrine the men would be toweling down and darting eyes at him while he combed his black hair. One of the men in particular named Yale who was from California interested Robin. He was well over six feet and built like a basketball player. His constant companion was a queen named Lacy who wasn't too good looking. This one day Lacy remarked to Robin as he was combing his hair in the latrine mirror, that Yale wanted his body. Yale toweling down just smiled and Robin smiled back knowingly. They met on occasion passing on the way to and from Spring Lake. He would do his laundry there and have his laundry bag strung over his broad shoulder. He was shy about asking Robin for some time. There was another one named Hernandez who didn't hesitate to ask. On one day Robin was in the office latrine where he worked and Hernandez also worked. Robin was combing his hair again and Hernandez walked in and remarked that he knew how much Robin wanted to kiss him. Robin continued combing his hair and nonchalantly threw an eye his way and replied, I think its the other way around. He never recovered from his embarressment on that one. He just couldn't jeoprodize his hetrosexuality by going out any further on this limb. Robin also had eyes for a bodybuilder named Spade who worked out in the barracks near his bunk. They shared the same area since their bunks touched.

Robin would many a night lay dreaming of Spade's arms around him. It seemed it was always the the wrong types who were brave enough to approach Robin. One night Robin returned to find his bedsheets and pillows missing from his bunk. This he suspected was the work of Pratka and Marcus who were chiding Robin earlier for not lifting weights. Marcus was a jealous closet queen and had had to get her frustrations out of her fat system. Robin found his bedding on the roof. Robin retrieved them and approached Spades bunk, the barracks were dark and the men were all asleep. Robin went over to where Spade lay and rubbed and caressed his bulging bicep, pretending to be concerned about the bedding and who was responsible. Robin called to him in a soft voice and he turned to him awaking and with his eyes opened sleepily asked what Robin wanted. Robin, in his best cry baby voice, asked who was responsible for the bedding caper. Spade just replied, "not me man." Robin kept his hand on Spade's bicep and didn't bother to remove it, and replied that he was going to have to go through the chain of command to get some results. He then returned to his bunk dreaming of Spade and what could have occurred. Spade would often tease Robin about his hair primping in the latrine while he was toweling down. Robin knew he wanted him. Spade was shorter than Yale but more muscled from his constant weightlifting he had light brown hair and very deep blue eyes. Robin was always taken back by his blue eyes which were very intense. While in the dayroom one night Robin and Rick were accosted by two spanish men in the unit. One was tall and good looking while the other was short and rather ugly. The good looking one approached Robin and the other one approached Rick They even locked the door after them when they entered the room. Robin and Rick were quite astounded by their quick agressive approach. Rick was

6

going to have none of this ugly one so he opened the door and ran down the stairs. Robin was left alone with the other one who was really quite cute. He pulled Robin over to sit on his lap and kissed him fully on the mouth. He tried to undue the shorts Robin was wearing and that's when Robin made a hasty exit.

Rick and Robin arrived at a roller rink called Skatetown. They had on some new outfits and the music was blaring and they were raring to go. Robin and Rick spun around the rink to the tune of "Kind Of A Drag" and "I Fought The Law," just in time to skate around the room with them, were Jerry and Sylvester. No one suspected that they were in their own drag. Robin loved the way Jerry's muscular arm felt around her waist. Rick and Sylvester were so close together their wheels almost caught. Rick saw her teenage friend another Jerry, sitting in the lounge area. She was too caught up with Sylvester to be concerned. Sylvester sqeezed Rick's plump buttocks as they rounded a turn. Demorest waved to Robin and she waved back. The number was over and they all converged to the lounge area. Demorest took Robin's hand and gave her a deep , long romantic look. Teenage Jerry came over and gave Rick a pat on on her behind. Jerry asked Rick to skate around the rink when the next number came on. She let him lead her on to the floor. Demorest took Robin onto the floor also and held her tightly to him like he never did before. The others just watched from the lounge area. Things went on like this for the rest of the evening until it was time to go. Rick asked Robin if she wanted to go on to the Holiday Inn where Carla and the rest of the crowd were sure to be found. They all decided to go and they took a cab from the rink to the hotel. They arrived after Marty Baker did. Marty was sure to hold a a little party afterwards. He had a little house just off Bragg blvd. The song on the juke box was slow and Jerry took Robin in his arms and began to dance. Sylvester did the same with Rick while Demorest could only wait for the next dance with Robin. Robin thrilled to Jerry's kiss on her neck while they danced to the seductive music. Robin didn't care if she ever left Ft Bragg if this would continue. They all gathered at the booth with Carla , Marty, Samantha and Wayne. Marty was telling the group about his German heritage. He said their name was the Von Bakers mind you. He said he was wearing something of a familly heirloom on a chain. Nobody believed him of course but he was so dramatic and convincing that they found it to be entertaining. Carla talked about taking a trip tomorrow to Charlotte and the Blue Note Lounge. She wanted to party with the friends that they had made their. Babs entered the club with her boyfriend, this big handsome hunk. No one knew howhow she managed to hang onto this number. They were a steady item for the last three months. God kows what she did with him in her little room on base. She and he sat down to join the others. Horn was on the phone again to of course, his lover in California. Horn was a recent newcomer to the group. He was in Robin's company. Rick couldn't stand Horn or for that matter not too many of the others. Robin just barely tolerated him.

The two of them entered the red room and soon did see Phil and Fleming seated at a table in conversation. They joined them and Phil said they just had dinner at the diner where May worked. Phil went on to say that May was complaining about her estranged hubby again. She was of course fed up with it all and threatening to return to Michigan. Robin listened for a bit to this and saw a familiar face at the bar. It was a blonde hunk named Steve she had met a few months back. He had a friend with him and soon they asked the girls to dance. Steve said that he and his friend had rented a room and wanted to know if they would like to join them in the room for some drinks. The two girls agreed and they decided to spend the night with the two guys. Champagne was flowing and Robin was soon in the arms of Steve dancing around the room to the tune of Blue Autumn. Steve said that he had thought of her often after they had last been together and that he wanted to see more of her. He held her tightly and kissed her lips tenderly. Robin responded and let her self melt into his burlly arms. Carla and Chuck danced with their champagne glasses in hand. That night Robin lay in Steve's muscular arms and he kissed her deeply and passionately. The moon was bright and could be seen through the window. The warm wind blew gently and you could hear the leaves rustle. Robin thought that she would like this to last longer.

Rick's job around the post was that of a troop leader, he led the reqruits around to their processing points. Robin was one of the people who processed them. The men didn't seem to mind either one of them. Robin entered the mess line for lunch and several of the men were jostleing into position to get behind her for some contact. This day after arriving at food station, one of the crew was taken back by her perfume. No one else seemed to mind the smell. Robin ate and was leaving the building when to her surprise she encountered a formation. The men were being led by someone she knew and he led them into loud whistles. She had to laugh at that and thought how amusing it was. Her friend had never shown her any romantic interest before. Rick led her troops into the office where Robin worked and Robin would type up their military records. Rick had a room in the same barracks as her troops. She would single out any one that she fancied and let him know that she was interested. This led to more than a few affairs. She had the nerve to complain how much she hated being in the army. Rick met this one troop named Tom who she fell head over heels in love with. She would invite him to her room for some long necking sessions. When she wanted someone she went after it with wild abandon. She would pick on the man she wanted and assign him to extra duty so that she could spend time alone with him. When it came time for Tom to leave Rick was almost panic stricken. She wanted to know where he was assigned to next so that she could look him up.

Rick saw Tom off when it came time for him to leave and she promised to visit him soon when she was discharged. Rick had two more months to go on her enlistment and was looking forward to returning to civilian life. She had a bad time of it in Korea with the cold weather and some of the people she had been assigned with. She would complain about the black men she had to serve with. She hated the way they went after the Korean girls and laughed about their sexual escapades. The girls were afraid of the blacks because of the size of some of them compared to their small equipment. Rick and Robin talked of this and that and decided to go to the Dixie restaurant for some breakfast of grits and eggs. Robin had never eaten grits before coming to the south. Robin put a quarter in the juke box for Nancy Sinatra's song Summer Wine. She did this and noticed that Yale had entered the place. She loved the way he lumbered in the room so broad shouldered and tall. He came over and sat down next to her. This was surprising to Robin for they had hardly spoken to each other before. He looked deeply into Robin's brown eyes with his own and came on very strongly say the least. He made no bones about how he wanted her. Robin was starting to get flushed from this attention and Rick found it amusing. Rick's attention was soon diverted to Demorest who was sitting over in the far corner. Rick motioned him over to join them which he did.

He said hello to Robin and Yale who were in the same barracks. Rick sqeezed his hand very provocatively and he flinched. Rick then laid his hand on his outstreched leg which gave him another start. Rick truly saw possibilities with this one. This made her forget how much she missed Tom for the time being. Yale asked Robin to go to the day room to watch tv that evening. Robin accepted his invitation and they left the Dixie together. Rick didn't seem to mind being alone with Demorest. She had plans for him that evening which he didn't know about yet. When Robin and Yale arrived at the dayroom they were pleased to find themselves alone. Yale turned on the set and sat down very close to Robin. He asked her if she were comfortable and then kissed her tenderly on the mouth. She let him take her into his strong arms and give herself to his sweet kisses. Robin loved the way he held her and rubbed his hand on her body. The tv was playing the Monkees but they weren't too concerned with what was playing. The golden autumn leaves were evident outside the window. It was truly a lovely evening for love.

Robin thought she'd like to stay longer than the time she had left in the army. Rick couldn't wait to get back to California to the land she thought no one should ever leave. She couldn't understand anyone wanting to live anywhere else. Robin had never been there so couldn't comprehend how she felt about the place. Rick wanted to stop by the theater where her teenage friend Jerry worked. He was on duty today and she greeted him in the lobby. He was on a break so they went up in the balcony area. Robin found a seat and decided to watch a movie. They were playing Matt Helm in Murderer's Row. Jerry and Rick were in the balcony area and Rick planted a kiss on his lips for starters. Jerry grabbed Rick and pulled him to his hard sixteen year old body. Rick squeeled with delight at this maneuvor and was besides herself with joy. Robin couldn't quite understand why she was attracted to someone ten years her junior. The movie ended and they went on to the skating rink. They met Carla and she said she was on her way meet some of her gang but that she could change her plans and go skating with them. She had just been at the restaurant where May worked. May was upset with her husband again and telling anyone who would listen. They arrived at the rink and changed in to their new outfits in the restroom. The place was jumping again and they played their favorite songs to skate to. Robin spotted the blonde hunk she had met earlier on the bus and he was coming her way. He grabbed her to him and they skated off to the sounds of "Coming On Strong." Rick saw Sylvestor and they also skated off. The lights were low and colored spotlights came on along with the big spinning mirrored ball that reflected all the different colors. Robin and her man were close and kissing in this romantic atmosphere. Rick wasted no time with Sylvestor. Carla met someone and was being whisked around the rink by this huge guy that was much bigger than she was. Three couples were close together side by side and they smiled at each other. Every one of them was having a most romantically dizzy time. Robin kicked up her legs to the beat and Rick shook her butt to the sound.

That same night later when they returned from an outing, they were accosted by a very amorous Cedeno. He beckoned for one or both of them to come over to where he was standing. Rick approached him and he promply

12

exposed himself and wanted action to say the very least. Rick was having none of this not in these very unprivate surroundings. Who knows who could walk in and get an eyefull. They all eventually parted company and settled down for the evening. Three days later Cedeno caught Robin alone in the latrine and pulled Robin to him in a most provacative manner. He kissed Robin hotly in the ear and whispered all the usual sweet nothings. Robin went on with what was a vain attempt at combing hair and washing one's face. Robin then turned around and suggested to Cedeno that he go into town and find someone to satisfy his urgency. Cedeno wouldn't let Robin go until Robin promised to meet him at his CQ duty station later that night. Robin promised him to be there, but of course had no intention of showing up. Robin went skating instead. Robin and Rick decided it was time to go out in feminine attire they were supposed to be males in society's eyes but to themselves and many amorous men they were strictly females. Rick wanted more action than he was getting which was ninety percent more than the average female gets. He thought trading in his levi cords for one night couldn't hurt. He convinced Robin that they needed a more womanly look. That Saturday morning the two of them walked from the company area to the main post. They arrived after acknowledging the usual whistles and cat calls on the way, which brightened up the trek.They met Demorest at the main post bus stop. Demorest boarded the bus with them and decided to join them later at skatetown after they finished their shopping. Robin received a loving glance from a blonde hunk across the aisle. He asked for Robin's name and was promptly told with a radient smile. He said that he liked Fort Bragg except for the lack of females. Robin gave him another smile which caused him to visibaly flush. He was truly the shy type and Robin loved

13

that. He then asked what Robin was doing that evening and Robin said that they were going roller skating at skatetown. He thought that a good idea and asked if he could join them. Rick by then had started a conversation with a black haired blue eyed airborne ranger and it looked as if they were about to start a little petting. His name was Sylvester and was just as handsome as the blonde hunk that Robin was talking with. This little interlude didn't stop Demorest from trying to win the conversation back from the blonde boy. Demorest was intending to be the only man to be involved with Robin that evening. He wasn't about to share Robin's attention or affection that night.

Robin and Rick decided to go out in full drag   They really didn't need to for their femininity was all too evident in regular clothes. That saturday morning the two of them walked to the main post area. They arrived at the bus stop to take the bus into Fayetteville. They acknowledged the usual whistles and cat calls along the way. They met up with Demorest at the bus staion, and he gave them a warm hello and they did the same. He assked if they were going roller skating at skatetown as he had planned to also. They told him they were going there. They got on the bus and sat at the rear. They always it seemed managed to sit near the cutest hunks. Robin was directly across the aisle from a well muscled airborne troop. He was in his uniform with the wings insignia on his chest. He gave Robin a blonde and blue eyed smile and she returned her brown eyed one. He then asked her how she liked Bragg and she said that it was better than some of the posts she had been on. He said that it was okay except for the lack of females. She then gave him another radiant smile which caused him to flush. He was the strong shy type which she loved. He asked what her plans were that evening and she told him. He She asked

14

if he would like to join like to join them in skating. Rick by this time had struck up a conversation with a black haired blue eyed airborne ranger. His name was Sylvester and really quite a number. Demorest was commenting on on this and that trying not to be left out of the involvement. Robin liked Demorest but this new guy was exciting to her. Demorest got of the bus to run some errand or another He said he would be at the skating rink later in the evening. Robin wa a little taken back by Demorest's behavior toward her. She did't know that he cared so much. The girls decided to shop a little before they went skating. They got off on Hay street, Fayetteville's main drag. The browsing began from shop window to shop window and ocassionaly entering to browse some more. They settled on this little shop that had some cute girly attire in the window. They picked out some numbers that would set off their their figures and legs. Robin picked out a baby blue skating outfit that fit perfectly and Rick found a yellow number that went well with her golden hair. They were bound to have a hot night in Carolina that night. They left the store and went up the street a little further to their favorite hamburger place. They each ordered a burger and coke float. Outside the window the hordes of men walked by. It certainly gave a girl an advantage here with forty thousand hungry men about. Robin thought it was a little bit of romantic heaven here. There certainly more opportunities for meeting someone.

Horn was always getting into his little plastic roles He pursued this hunk named Yale to no end. He even asked Robin to look into his file to find out his middle name to tease him about it. Demorest asked Robin to dance and held her tighter than before he asked if she would let him be his date for the rest of the evening. Robin said that she wouldn't promise him anything. The crowd began to break up and Marty announced the little get together at his place. They went in several cars. The guests included a couple of of serjeants in full uniform. Waynetta was sitting in the front seat next to one of these serjeants. The two of them couldn't have been sitting any closer. Waynetta was exhibiting the most seductive behavior in her arsenal of charms. Her legs were crossed very feminely and her arms were all over the man   At every red light they kissed very provocatively and they did this with wild abandonment. Robin and Jerry watched from the back seat and Samantha did the same from the front. Rick had her hands full in another car. They all arrived at Marty's place and soon couples were forming all over the place. They were scattered haphazardly on the furniture and on the living room rug. Marty went to her bedroom and dragged a number with her. She soon emerged in the nude and made a quick check on the furnace, to do this she got down on all fours with her business in the air. She replaced the floor vent and grabbed a drape and performed a little dance. She sometimes would fake suicide attempts during her little dramatic episodes   During these dramas she had everyone convinced that she would cut her wrists. How could they forget the night her mother arrived. She was banging on the door just as everyone had settled down with his mate. Her mother never had suspected her son got into drag attire. She had a pass key and she burst in on the scene drunk and beleagured. She was also quite belligerant and vocal when she summed up the situation that greeted her   She cursed everyone out for five minutes before someone shouted her down. Marty grabbed her by her flaming red hair and shoved her out the front door and promptly bolted it. Marty then turned up the music and they all began to dance like nothing had happened. This time however Marty's mother was nowhere in sight. Demorest and Robin would sit and neck for a while , and then Jerry would take over the duties. Rick comforted Sylvester over in a corner of the living room. One of the older queens who happened to be in uniform, and from Robin's unit, was walking around checking out who was with whom and their identities. This would make good conversation for at least a few days. Carla was with her Italion stallion Valluchi. She was absolutely pawing all over the poor guy. Valluchi called her his little Gigi. Mickey was carrying on involved in a wild dance number in the middle of the floor. She was of course in full makeup with her hair dyed red this week, her commander will die on Monday when he sees it.

Carla called Robin at her duty station and asked her if she would like to the NCO club that evening. Robin said that she would love to go and that they would meet at the old division snack bar. When Robin walked in she found Carla sitting in a corner. Carla was wearing a red turtle neck sweater almost the same color as her hair. She had her hair straightened and dyed and combed over one eye. Carla said she felt like crawling into the woodwork because so many men were staring at her. She was chain smoking and drinking a beer. Robin got herself a colt forty five and they began to discuss the latest events around the fort. Carla told Robin that Mickey would be getting out and going back to New York city in a few months. She also mentioned a serjeant who had a place in Puerto Rico and that they were invited there for a visit. She went on to say that this queen named Rosemary was involved in a little accident the other day. It seemed that she had been running from this group of spanish soldiers who were trying to get to her. She started to run and darted in front of a bus. She wasn't injured but was pretty shaken up to say the least. She was fed up with

17

the military life and was thinking of telling them her story. She was involved with a Lieutenant and they talked of running off together somewhere. She wanted to get a sex change and marry the officer. Everyone was shocked to think that she would tell them her story. Carla and Robin finished their drinks and headed for the NCO club   They ran into some men from Carla's unit and this one in particular was asking Carla about a wac that she knew and if Carla would introduce him to her. Carla told him that she was gay and wouldn't be interested in him. He didn't seem to mind that and pressed on. Carla said she would see what she could do.   The girl accepted his offer to dance and Robin and Carla accepted two other offers to join two guys at their table. The guys offered to take them to their barracks and they accepted. They had a camaro and it was fast as they drove on. The boys wanted to park and neck a while first so the girls agreed and the kisses and hugs were flowing and outside the autumn wind was blowing, it was an idyllic evening to say the least. The guys wanted to see them again so they promised to meet at the club tomorrow night. Carla returned to her barracks and went to her locker to put away her clothes and get ready for bed. She was startled to see a pair of panties hanging in side the door of the locker. She knew that they were teasing her and she wasn't concerned because she knew how to handle them.

Demorest had to get off the bus and he promised to see them all later that evening. Robin felt excited about meeting this hunk named Kirk, but was a little surprised by Demorest and his reaction. He had never before revealed so much about his feelings. Robin thought that he was no more than a passing fancy in Demorest's life. He did have a girlfriend back home and was planning on getting married soon. Robin and Rick got off the bus on Hay street. They

18

immediately began browsing and the shop windows proved interesting. Fayetteville had a nice selection of shops and department stores for a city of its size. They found a little shop where they could get their skating outfits. Robin loved a darling baby blue number it was cut high and would show off the legs. Robin got a rush after trying it on. Rick found a yellow one cut equally short. The two of them would knock the place over that night. Rick knew the kind of things that they could get into when they got into these. They were certainly going to be looking forward to a hot night in Carolina. They went up the street further and stopped in their favorite hamburger place. They each had a burger and a coke float. Rick had introduced Robin to coke floats. This among many other things was a California favorite according to Rick. They observed the men passing on Hay street and it certainly was heaven here for a girl. It seemed that all forty thousand men were out looking for action. There weren't that many eligible females in town, especially one of this size. Rick didn't think Fayetteville could hold a candle to L.A. but Robin had no complaints having lived in Rochester, N.Y. with all of its drabness. Robin loved it here and wanted to stay on longer than the seven months of his tour of duty. Robin and Rick headed back to the base to get dressed in Rick's room where they would at least have some privacy. They had planned on leaving at seven. They shaved their legs and applied their makeup. They teased their hair and put on thse little hairpieces to make their hair look longer. Their efforts proved to be smashing and they couldn't wait for the reaction they would get from the men on post and off. As soon as they got outside Rick's room they heard the whistles start. They passed a formation and received an ovation. By the time they got to the main post area there were a hundred different men howling to them. When they finally got on the bus they met Carl and he recognized them immediately. Carl became all excited in their attire and was just bublling over with joy. He said he was on his way to meet his friends Babs and Rosemary, Phil and of course Fleming. They all met at a restaurant on Hay street .They had their favorite waitress wait on them and they exchanged gossip. The three of them went to the restaurant and ran into two others Horn and Mickey.

Carla met Rosemary, Tina and Mickey at Marty's place of employment a motel, which he had a job as a desk clerk. This was a little motel on Bragg blvd. Since the boss had gone out of town, they had the whole place to them selves. Marty let them in and they wondered what mischief they would certainly get into. Carla walked to her private room. She had caught the attention of one of the clientel. He had a room and had his door open as Carla sashayed by. He caught Carla's little trot and read something into it. She looked at him with her best I don't give a dam look. He knew what that meant, and dragged her into his room. She naturally put up her resisting act, no please , oh stop, what are you trying to do. She then lapsed into a love song as his big arms encircled her. She moaned and didn't even think about groaning as he placed his sweet kisses on her face and neck. She let him have his way and then started to fight for more when he stopped. She felt like whatever egyptian blood she had in her was about to boil and she was not about to let him take the kettle off. Rosemary and Tina had enough to keep them busy and you could hear the noise creeping down the hall. They had two boyfriends and one of them was a drill serjeant with hat and all. He said it was perfectly militarily acceptable to fraternize with the uniform on or off. Mickey and Marty were in the ballroom and of course they were attracted to the heavy red drapes. They got involved in a dance number and were wrapping the drapes around themselves and dancing to the rhythm. They were attracting the attention of two admirers These two had rented a room earlier and were absolutely shocked when Marty had burst into the room with her pass key. She was wearing a topless lace bathing suit she must have made from a curtain. The scene heated up when Mickey followed her entrance with one of her own. She was wearing a one piece number from another era. The guys were lounging in semi dress and liked what they witnessed after they had gotten over the initial shock. Mickey made the first move toward Ken a broad chested red head. She of course uttered her very famous , ooh honeee !. She was about to utter more when he grabbed her by the neck and everthying she tried to say got warbled. She managed a faint repeat of honee, when she was able to get her breath. Marty threw herself on top of Mike and let out a Tarzan yell or in her case scream.

North Carolina hadn't seen the likes of this in the past nor would they in the foreseeable future. Samantha had a little spat with Waynetta and proceeded to bit into the child's rhinestone studded earlobe. Waynetta threw her magnolia bouquette and hit Samantha in the beehive. These two were supposed to be best friends. Carla got involved with a stud from the twenty sixth artillary battalion, where they were both stationed. He was wooing and cooing her to her wildest of withering heights. She looked as if she had been lost to some eerie abandonment. To add insult to all of this injury, who would arrive, but Waynetta's hillbilly to say the least, mother. She upon recognizing her son-daughter in drag, let out a scream in full throttle B flat, queers, quarrs!!! She couldn't seem to get the pronounciation correct. She sniffled into her woolworth's

21

hankerchief. "My son !! What have you done to my son!! Waynetta was rather disheveled by the many attacks on her virtue by the unruly men at the party led her mother to be even more upst. Meanwhile bodies in all sorts of attire and unattire, were scrambling to get out at any available exit. Carla left the party and went on to Marty Baker's house. Wayne and Sam and a few of the others at the party followed. The next morning Carl was late in getting up. He rubbed his tiny eyelids and pulled on his fatigues over his bikini underwear the same underwear he wore in basic training while lying on his bunk and rubbing his legs with nair, to the shock of the other recruits in his barracks. He caught the look of one fellow named George, who was concluding his lusty estimation of Carl's dressing routine. He was remembering a previous scene that occurred in the furnace room of another building. Carl hurried to the mess hall and had some french toast and hot coffee. He wondered if life would be this exiting after his discharge. There couldn't possible be this many available men around. One thing he wouldn't miss was his relationship with his first serjeant. This left every thing to be desired. He could get on his case with alarming regularity. He wondered what kind of tongue lashing he had in store for him today. He wanted him to read off the roster to him to see about someone who was awol. Carl rushed outside to the hastily formed formation and began reading off names to see who was missing. The formation was as as hastily put together as Carl's makeup. His touch and glow was all touch and no glow. The men didn't seem to notice as they gave their pin up girl a loud array of whistles. Carl caught the smiling faces of more than a few of her affairing partners. Carl picked up the roster and began calling off the names, at the conclusion of this when the formation was breaking up, he felt the press and the crush of bodies against his own. He

22

giggled his way to the orderly room.

Robin met Carl. Carl belonged to a clique who broke every rule the army made it seemed. One in this group was an ex New York hairdresser named Mickey. Mickey had a tendency to change his haircolor as often as there were inspections. To the company commander this was totally unacceptable and he was determined to do something about it. One day in the mess hall he accousted Mickey about his current haircolor which was of an argueable color, the closest color it resembled was that of a plum. As the commander was reprimanding Mickey he was taken back by the contents of Mickey's tray, which was thrown all over the commander. Mickey was busted for this affair, but he had gotten away with so much more before this. There was the time Mickey lined up a group of trainees in the barracks where he had a room. He ordered the trainees to drop their shorts for a short arm inspection. This they did promptly without hesitation. Mickey's friends nicknamed Tina and Rose Mary arrived as this had proceeded to an embarrassing state of affairs for the trainees much to the delight of Mickey and his friends. Carl and his group threw a terribly illegal party one night under the moonlit Carolina pines. The MP's were called and by the time they had arrived the participants were in various states of dress or undress and scattering in all directions. Carl managed his escape by being carried by this hunk up to the second floor room he occupied. Carl and his group rented a house in town to have among other things parties. There were to be plenty of these to follow, one in particular involved two civilian boys named Sam and Wayne. They were done up in complete drag and Sam or Samantha as they called him , was in a pink chiffon number topped off by a beehive hairdo. Wayne or Waynetta, was done up in very southern style lace like a belle on the veranda of an ante-bellam mansion. He topped this off with a mantea and a magnola blossom in the area behind a rinestone studded ear lobe. Well the boys from the base had arrived that they had invited and they carried on to heights this crew had reached many times before. Couples were forming two and sometimes three, involved were "many styles of dress and fashion." from rigid military to southern debutante drag, to wac drawers minus the skirt!! Carla was nowhere to be seen. He was given to late arrivals and dramatic ones at that. After several hours of this madness, Carla finally arrived. He was wearing what looked like had been a velvet drape from Tara. He was wearing so much jewelry it was difficult to find his tiny features. The glare off them was nearly blinding. He opened the door and tried to play down his appearance by uttering a very simply but barely audible "hello how are you". He knew he had to play down what he looked like because nothing he said could quite equal it. Well after he settled in and they could get somewhat used to his rather garrulous appearance, the party really took off.

The first serjeant asked Carl what was so funny, he seemed to have the impression that Carl was keeping things from him to say the least. Robin called and wanted to know if Carl would like to go to the Dragon club on base. Carl agreed to go along, thinking something interesting might occur. Carl arrived at Robin's barracks and found Robin combing out his blue black hair. Carl had on his tightest white jeans, Robin meanwhile had on a pair of figure hugging burgundy cord shorts and a green velour pullover. Carl wondered what else would be hugging that figure tonight. Carl was taken back by a cute hunk named Spade entering the latrine. His eyes roamed up and down Robin while Robin nonchalantly went about his business of getting ready. The two of them left the barracks and headed to the main post area that the club was located. The trees had begun to change and it looked quite lovely. There were several hunks jogging and they waved as they went by. There was a football game going on at the field nearby and the snackbar had music blaring outside,   inside men were playing pinball and pool. Carl was thinking red tonight and was in the mood for a redhead. Robin had his mind on blonde. They entered the club and found Phil and Mickey seated at a table. Phil had on his hairpiece and it looked a bit fluffy. Mickey screamed his hellos and Phil offered a more subdued greeting. Phil had mentioned that his best friend Fleming had just re-inlisted and collected a sizeable bonus for doing so. He was wondering if maybe he should do the same, it certainly was a tempting offer. Robin and Carl thought about it also and it didn't seem like such a bad idea. Carl wondered what he would do with 10,000.00 dollars, maybe buy a new corvette. While Carl thought about this, a red head over in the corner thought about other things. Carl caught his glance and smiled back. He came over to the table and introduced himself to Carl and sat down. He said he was from San Francisco and Carl lit up on that. Robin spied a blonde hunk over at the bar, Robin went over to order some drinks and see what else might occur. The blonde asked what Robin's name was and one thing led to another and soon he was heading back to the table with Robin. Robin wanted so badly to slow dance with him, but that wouldn't go over so well here. He held Robin's hand under the table and pressed his leg against Robin's. They all looked up as Babs and his hunk walked to the bar, Babs wasn't letting him get to far away. The music played one of their favorites as they felt their drinks kick in.Carla felt her hand being caressed by the redhead and the wine cooler.

25

Carla was late in getting up today after getting in late last night. She was out on another one of her jaunts, these would occur at a regular pace. She rubbed her tiny eyelids and pulled on her fatigues over her bikinin underwear. She caught the look of George Lern as he he summed up his lusty estimation of her body . Carly merely dismissed this as all in a days work. Lern was apparently thinking of other scenes that had occurred in the furnace room. Carla hurried to the mess hall and had her french toast and hot coffee. She was thinking of what Robin had told her last night about going to miss this place, she did have to admit that that things had heated up quite a bit since her arrival. She wondered if life in California would be this exciting. Well one thing for sure she wouldn't miss her first serjeant and his behavior towards her. He seemed to be getting on her case with alarming regularity. She wondered what kind of tongue lashing he had in store for her today. She arrived back at the orderly room to begin the day's work. The first serjeant came in and told her to read of the roster. It seemed there had been a few awols over the weekend. Carla rushed out to the hastily assembled formation. It looked as hastily assembled as her makeup. Her touch and glo was all touch and no glo. The men didn't seem to notice her ill prepared face. They gave her a hearty welcome with not a few whistles. Carla caught the smiling faces of a few of her tricks and treats. Carla picked up the roster from the podium and began to call off the names. She then gave over the podium to the serjeant and he warned any of them against going awol. As the formation came to an end, Carla was caught in the throng of eager bodies pressed against hers. She giggled her way back to the orderly room. The serjeant came in and saw her face and asked what was so funny. She replied that she didn't know quite what had

26

come over her.

Robin and Rick stopped by the motel after they had heard from May at the restaurant that some little affair was taking place. They were as usual in top form with the tightest jeans and velour pullovers on. Their hair was styled and sprayed to the limits. Carla of course had to remark on how well the two were looking. She proceeded with her usual , "how are you", spoken with her flawless theatrical flair. Rick and Robin said that they needed a drink. Mickey staggered around to the bar area and mixed up a few drinks for the queens. Robin wanted a margarita and Rick had a Shirley Temple. The rum reminded Mickey of her homeland. One wondered how she could make a drink when she certainly couldn't handle another one. Marty could be heard moaning from a strange part of the room she was in. She was under the bed and her last mate was nowhere to be found. Horn by this time had also arrived and he was joined by Waynetta, the bee hive girl herself, Samantha was also in tow. Samantha was shocked to see an old acquaintance coming out of one of the rooms. She told Waynetta that a girl just never knew who she would run into next. Robin and Rick were starting to get some attentive looks from some of the guys. Rick was in her usual blonde splendor, she looked as if she had stepped out of a field of wheat. Robin kept telling her that she looked so very very vogue. Rick called Robin Miss Night and Robin called her Miss Day in return. Rick would sometimes flinch at this sometimes. She wasn't fond of Doris Day.

Mickey was fit to be tied, and Rosemary didn't help matters either. Marty's boss rang up and said that he was going to stop in later. Mickey took the call and said that Marty was busy, the boss thought that Marty was showing somebody a room. Mickey slurred speech didn't tip him off that there was something going on that shouldn't be. He decided against coming out to see how things were. Marty finished off her cannibal dance and took off very quickly to find a new mate. She announced over the pa system for every man to line up for inspection. She said that she was not going to take no for an answer. She threatened to use her pass key if necessary. Carla arrived at the lounge area and mentioned to Mickey that Marty was the craziest bitch she had ever encountered. The few men that did come out for inspection were shocked to see this madwoman in a drill serjeants hat preparing to line them up for an inspection. She looked pretty amusing and not the least bit official in her get up. No one took her very seriously as she proceeded to try and inspect the goods. She even had a whip as she demanded compliance to her orders. The day was saved when one man dragged her into one of the rooms. Babs arrived and couldn't believe her eyes at Marty's escopades. Marty didn't even acknowledge her prescence, but Carla had her eyes locked on the hunk that was with Babs. Babs wasn't amused by Carla's seductive look at her beloved.

Robin looked radiant in an olive green velour top with white levi shorts. The shorts complimented her shapely tanned legs. When Robin made an appearance at Carla's barracks earlier, someone asked if Robin was a rock star or some celebrity. Carla of course said that she was a celebrity, and Robin was amused by this when Carla told her later. Carla joined the two girls by the bar area and was taken aback by Robin's Elizabeth Taylor like beauty. Carla passed on her reflection to Robin and Rick squinted her eyes in distaste, she was used to garnering up all the attention. Marty added to the confusion of the place by appearing out of nowhere with very little on. She was making a pit stop to get a drink. The girls burst out laughing at Marty's disheveled demeanor. Mickey was heard cackling in her stuupor state. She had seen Marty this way many many times before. Rosemary and Tina rushed over to see what the laughing was about. This was not a scene out: of a William Inge play, like Picnic, it was more like Motel Hell. The girls were certainly raising enough of it and tonight was no exception. Horn was nowhere to be seen, he must have been locked in a room or left altogether. He told everyone he couldn't wait to get to California and his lover aboard their fabulous houseboat, mind you. He and Marty used to trade their yarns at the Stein room, in the Holiday Inn. Marty of course would fill every ear with her Von Baker heritage tales.

A few moths ago, before this affair at Marty's place of work, Rick was at the bar at the Prince Charles and having a chat with Phil and Fleming. They were fast friends who didn't take too much to others. They had once invited Robin for dinner at May's place and failed to show up. They didn't even bother to apoligize afterwards. Phil and Fleming walked through the front door of the motel and didn't even bother to acknowledge the prescence of Rick or Robin or anyone else for that matter. They simply went over to the bar and instructed Mickey on the matter of their drinks. Robin saw her old friend Steve and he came to where she was sitting. Marty's mother and Wayne's mother were finally thrown out of the place and it took several people to do it. Mickey had helped throw out Wayne's mother by first knocking off her pillbox hat. She in turn called Mickey a brown quarr. Babs with all of her heftiness wrestled the two women to the front door then everyone gave them the final heave to the sidewalk. Carla by this time had made her final move to Bab's hunk of a boyfriend. He had asked her to dance after she had sent so many signals his way. He encircled her petite form by his own very husky one. He loved her proud full behind and caressed it much to her delight. Babs was now entering the lounge and looking for him. When she saw him dancing with Carla she let out a scream similiar to the one Marty's mother had made when she had entered the motel. She rumbled towards Carla like the engine of a very big freight train.

Carla caught a glimpse of Babs out of the corner of her eye and let out a scream. Bab's boyfriend had his back towards Babs and didn't know what had hit them as this train rolled in. Carla fell backwards towards Mickey. Carla had a dazed look in her semi slanted eyes as she looked up at Mickey, who had caught her just as she was about to hit the floor. Carla felt nothing like the farmers daughter, whom she loved to watch on tv. Although she went to catholic high, there wasn't a trace of catholic on her face as she looked at Babs. When she was in high school, being gay was so taboo. Her mother had found a love note she had written to a boy in school and wanted an explanation from her. Carla said it was notes from a play they were doing. Her mother of course wasn't buying that one. Carla went into the army rather apprehensively. She was really enjoying the scenery at the physical and she caught quite a few looks herself especially her behind. Robin was in another lineup in Buffalo, where they had forced that poor child to go after induction. She of course was appalled at all of the nudity being displayed. Some of the men picked up on her and got respectively aroused. On the train from Buffalo to Ft Dix she got very depressed. She stayed in her cabin until some of the guys made her join them in the lounge for some drinks and conversation. She ended up in the quarters of a big burly blonde. She was ravaged that night as the train made its way through the lower Adarondacks. He covered her tears with hot kisses and had her protectively in his burly arms, soothing her painful journey.

They continued this way until dawn until the train made its way into NYC. She began that morning with a song in her heart and a man on her mind. Back to the motel fiasco Babs was somehow wrestled to the floor by none other than Mickey. She must have found the strength from that last grasshopper that she had. Carla smiled keenly at Babs as she hit the floor and she made an elephant like leap towards her. She was kept from her target by Mickey. Carla had left the dance floor and swiftly went over to talk to, Robin who had of course returned from her encounter. The two were chatting about sex changes and future life in California. Babs and Horn were from LA and of course so was Horn. Rick was the most outspoken about the California lifestyle and was trying to lay this on everyone. Marty came into the lounge area and announced that she required a Vodka stinger especially after the stinging reunion she had with her mama. The two heiffers, Martyy's and Wayne's respective mothers, went on to Bragg blvd to do some late shopping. Samantha arrived looking for her best friend Waynetta and she was looking spunky in her french twist hairdo. She had been over at teacher's house, as they referred to their teacher friend Jon. He loved young boys and threw parties that would have outraged any community, let alone Fayetteville. May had phoned , and wanted someone to go searching the bars with her for her scoundrel husband. Marty and Waynetta compared experiences with their irate mothers while sipping their drinks.

Horn was now in the others prescence at the lounge area. He was occupado in one of the rooms with somebody or other. He surely must have told the person that he was from California. With all the rest of his tired life story. Robin and Rick asked Mickey to fix them another drink. Robin had a Margarita again and Rick switched to a sloe gin fizz. Marty just opened her mouth and fizzed. She was on another break she couldn't hold out much longer they thought. Maybe it was the pep pills she sometimes took or the aphrodosiac that Mickey had put in her drink. Tina and Rosemary wanted Vodka stingers and Mickey squealed in her eagerness to fix them. The party was reeling and rolling and somebody had the nerve to put money in the juke box to make it rock. Thompson came from somewhere and grabbed Marty from her barstool. She let out her Jane yell and everyone perked up. They all started to dance to the music and the chattering picked up a bit. Tina and Rosemary were doing the latest cool jerk, and Robin and Rick were doing the pony. The song was "Up Tight" and soon every one was doing the jerk. Horn snapped at Mickey when she stepped on his foot by mistake. Mickey gave him a shot to the midsection in her drunken form. Her cover girl was now beginning to cake and she was in no condition to make repairs. She looked as if she was about to hit the floor along with her makeup. One wondered what was holding her up. Her purple hair seemed to be taking on a new shade. Robin put another dime in the juke box and played Cool Jerk.

Carla jerked herself into a frenzy and her straightened hair nearly broke off in the process. Robin and Rick were vibrating Carla got carried away in her dancing and took off her sweater and in the process swiped the side of Marty's

32

face. Marry retaliated by striking Carla with one her beringed fingers. This one of course contained a rare jewel from Germany. By this time Mickey had to have another vodka stingers. She tried to do the jerk with that in her hand but that was almost impossible. Somebody said they had seen Marty's mother outside one of the windows, but they had to be kidding, no one could handle another one of her scenes. She, according to Marty had met Waynetta's mother for the first time the other day. The possibility that they would come together to check on their children, was discussed. That would be enough to stop time , not to mention the good time they were having. Surely enough it was them together banging on the windows and screaming obcentities in their southern drawls. Marty's mother demanded to be let in and somebody obliged her. Marty was blind drunk and oblivious to her mother's prescence. Her mother had a few too many also. She ran to the lounge area in an almost frenzy, to get at Marty. Waynetta's mother. Waynetta's mother broke in between her and Samantha's cool jerk. Waynetta was almost too bombed to notice. She just bobbed like a cork when her mother jerked her off the dance floor.

You would have thought her hairdo would have gotten away from her from the force of the action. She let out a moan in southern b flat, oh maw!! Samantha in rare form took off after Waynetta's mother. She screamed a few obcentities of her own at her. Waynetta was by now toppling to the floor like a bean pole. Waynetta's mother was no better or worse than Marty's mother in these kind of situations. Marty was dancing with her friend to the song, "I'm your puppet." She looked like a puppet when her mother grabbed her by her skinny neck. She would have done Howdy Doody proud this night. One couldn't believe the force that woman put on Marty, it was like a Texas toranado, and Marty was in the eye of the storm. All you could see was her shoes flying off and her long painted toe nails. Her boyfriend was helpless to intervene. Marty's mother dragged Marty to the hallway and people came out of their rooms to see what was happening. Marty's mother screamed at them. Marty managed to escape and ran into an open room. This room was very much occupied and the water bed got even more choppy when Marty dived in. Marty's mother jumped in the bed after her and the couple on the bed broke apart and fled the scene in horror. Marty's mother wasn't the least bit concerned about intruding on their privacy, and neither was Marty. A heavyset couple came into the room and looked as if they were going to tear Marty and her mother apart. The big man had Marty pinned down on the floor and his lady friend had Marty's mother in a choke hold on the bed. Marty had lost all her jewelry in the fracas even her famous cameo necklace, with a very suspicious looking cameo that resembled her on it. Marty freed herself from the man only to be tackled by her mother again. Marty's manfriend came to her rescue and took her mother off her and set her aside. The hefty couple saw him and grabbed their hefty clothes and took off for the even her famous cameo necklace, with a very suspicious looking cameo that resembled her on it. Marty freed herself from the man only to be tackled by her mother again. Marty's manfriend came to her rescue and took her mother off her and set her aside. The hefty couple saw him and grabbed their hefty clothes and took off for the front door. Everyone came into the room to see if anyone had survived. Marty's high pitched screams made them think she was near death. Waynetta was of course creating sounds of her own in the lobby area. Her mother was slapping her face repeatedly and ruining her makeup in the process. She had laid down

34

her own version of Carolina law, and Waynetta could only reply in her spacey drawl. Her mother went on about Waynetta's promise not to get mixed up with these quarrs again. She went on about having to drag her out of the last party in that silly outfit and here she was doing it all over again. Waynetta's mother went on about how she didn't raise her son to be a quarr. She said they would just die at the society circle if they ever found out about all of this. Waynetta just looked at her mother in complete exasperation and and wondered just what the hell she was doing here. Horn's lover had arrived and wanted to know immediately where Georgie porgie was. He had just flown in from LA and wanted to see his beloved. He had visited here before and they had eaten at May's restaurant. May would always fill him in about Horn's activities. Horn was apparently involved with someone in one of the rooms. He after a long search found the right room where Horn was. He broke apart the twosome and Horn was left to explain his behavior.

Living up to his reputation as a liar, Horn said it was a harmless little fling. Eric had gotten wind of another one of Horn's indescretions, namely the bus driver. This had to do with the bus between Ft Bragg and Fayetteville and Horn's relentless pursuit of the driver. Horn would strike up a conversation and continue to ride the bus with the driver unlil the end of the run. He of course expected to go home with the driver. He was always shocked when the driver would say his goodbyes and be on his way. He would also pursue many guys in his company and wouldn't let up on some of them. Robin had run into several guys who would complain about Horn's aggressive behavior. Robin was in the old division area and happen to run into an old friend named Steve, they had a drink at the division watering hole and continued on to Steve's room in one of the barracks. As they entered the room, Robin's dark eyes glowed romantically and Steve's blue eyes smoldered with increased passion. They were filled with merriement and mischief. He had bulging biceps and he pulled Robin to him strongly. She let herself be swept away as he pressed her to his rockhard body. They kissed passionately and he fondled her erect rose buds. He rubbed her creamy silken skin and she caressed his bulging biceps. She rubbed her hands over the broad expanse of his chest. He marveled at her long shapely legs and and he kissed them lovingly. She tugged at the tufts of blond chest hair and let her hand be guided downward. He placed her in position and took her with a profound urgency.

She positioned herself and he took off on her famous runway. Marty by this time was wearing the hell out of her guy and needed her a replacement. She wasted little time in finding herself another. This one was from the eighty second airborne, and a squad leader corporal. She called him Thompson, she didn't even bother to ask him his first name. She just started to attack and undress him. He cried out his oohs and many ahs as this cow took him under the covers, and believe me she didn't come up for air. Mickey was off at the cocktail lounge getting stoned and dead drunk. The bar was closed for repairs but that didn't stop her from opening it up and making like a bartendress. She mixed one drink that took off like a hungry crocodile in the water. She squeeled with delight and beckoned for the crowd to join her. She yelled, "Marty honee," "Tina honee," and "Carla honeee," come and have a drink. Well Marty was too involved with Thompson to come this way but she certainly came the other way, and more than Once. Rosemary dragged herself away from her friend and asked

Mickey to fix her something good. Mickey obliged by giving her a wild turkey on the rocks, which she promptly gulped down. Mickey decided on a grasshopper for Marry and spiked it with a love potion, as if she needed one. "Marty honee," come and get your drinkee, she called out.

Marty was by this time thrown out of the room by Thompson, and she decided to find out why Mickey was yelling honee. You could hear her all over the motel. Well Marty arrived at the lounge area and took a look at a dead drunk, Mickey with questionable hair color and bartendress theatrics, and burst out laughing. She said "oh girl, "you belong in a Betty Grable movie", "but a pinup for the guys, you'll never be" Mickey simply squeeled with drunken delight and handed Marty her drinkee pooh. Marty took a few swallows and continued to chit chat in her famous manner. Her conversation usually centered on truck drivers and their truck stops. The rest areas were particularly noteworthy. She related how she had gotten trapped by the vice one night in her car. He propositioned her and she responded positively. He let her off the hook but she promply got on his. You couldn't pull them apart, so she said, but one wonders whether to believe her on that one. Mickey was getting anxious for the love potion to take effect on Marty. She didn't have long to wait. Marty bolted from the bar stool and ripped off a drape and wrapped herself in it. She began to undulate. This turned into an outright cannibal dance that no one there had seen the likes of, nor would they ever again probably.

Carla slapped her boyfriend and told him to continue, or else. He tried to grant her her wishes, but he was too pooped to pop. Carla threw one of her best Nefertitti fits and left the room. She had on an outfit that looked as if she had just posed for a calendar. She wiggled on down the hallway to see what else was up, for it was certain nothing in this room was. She landed another hungry GI, hopefully with more staying power than the last one. She wanted him desperately to zero in on her target area. She wasn't concerned in the least that he was a mere recruit. She was going to give him some very basic training. He took to her right away and they started the ritual. He told her that she looked exotic and that her skin had Indian red hues in it. She was really pleased by this and urged him to go on with his summary of her charms. She led his hand to her newly creamed legs and asked his opinion of those. He told her that they felt silken and slick as silver. His words came out in between the oohs and ahs as he ravaged her curves and crevices. She reveled in his description of her gams. He then ran his fingers through her newly straightened "Joey Heatherton" haircut. Even before Joey had it done. He said that her hair was soft as silk and twice as straight, almost as straight as he was. Something else was now straightening out, and Carla noticed without too much of a time lapse.

Robin and Carla, meanwhile were demonstrating the "hullaballo,jerk," and the "monkey" for anyone sober enough to appreciate them. Babs and her boyfriend had made up and were dancing real slow. Mickey, Tina, and Rosemary were talking hair, makeup, and clothes. Phil and Fleming were having a quiet discussion about Fieming's plans to reinlist and possibly take six more years. He wanted the ten thousand bonus and liked the army life, especially their brand of army life. Phil was all set to get out and return to Atlanta. Horn of course was going to California to live on the houseboat with his so called lover. Robin and Carla had finally stopped dancing and Carla went over to the bar and ordered her a black russian. She began relating to Robin her work update. It seems she had to go to the barracks and take inventory of all the mattresses and bunks that were not being used. After she had arrived in this one particular barracks, there was one man still in his bunk. Corporal Lern didn't have duty that day and was relaxing in his drawers. He observed with some interest,Carla sashaying into the barracks with clipboard in hand. Carla in turn noticed him and what he was not wearing. She wanted to respond to his looks accordingly, but decided to get on with what she was doing. He inquired about her task and then asked her to come closer. She edged cautiously closer and he said for him to get even closer. He made a lunge for her and she ran down the length of the barracks. He caught her and pinned her to the wall. She dropped her clipboard and he dropped his shorts.

She began her usual cries of no, no, no. He pressed against her and she melted into ectasy. This time she moaned yes, yes, and he smothered her with wet kisses. Her makeup was in shambles and her uniform was only half there. He told her in between kisses that he'd been wanting her for a long time. She said that she had noticed him and they got further involved. Next door they had a barracks for people who were caught in same sex encounters. They were awaiting their discharges. Some of them had become defiantly flamboyant and were openly pursuing more activity. Carla and Lern finally broke up and Carla was heading back to the orderly room. She looked up at the auspicious barracks and recognized a queen. Her name was Bobbie Jo. She had been caught in the act with another troop. She had been drafted in the army and of course was horrified at having to go in. But after a while things began to heat up for her sexually, she had many more possibilities for sexual encounters. She had a very high sex drive and this is what the doctor ordered. She got involved with some of the guards they deployed to keep order. It was hard to believe she was from Cleveland. She was named "Miss Gay Cleveland," at one of the gay bars. She used to perform and sing numbers in costume. Bobbie Jo was the leader in the Queen's barracks. She would get the others fired up in rebellion against military authority. She was quite a little "Jane Fonda" in that sense.

At the motel everything was winding down. Ail the military guys were heading back to the base.Carla, Robin, Rick, Horn, and Babs and Rosemary got into Bab's car and decided to check out Hay street. Carla swore she saw May chase her husband. The rest of the street was dead and everyone went home. When Carla arrived at her barracks she found another pair of panties hung over her locker. She took a look at the hunk on the top bunk, wondering if he was involved. She toossed that notion from her head and tossed her head defiantly and crawled under the covers. She bolted out of bed with her body covered with shaving cream. No one even stirred in their bunks but she could have sworn that she had heard some cackling. The man on the top bunk was snoring and she decided to have a little fun of her own and began to recklessly fondle him. He produced a rather noticable development and she acted accordingly. She could have cared less if anyone was watching and the man she was servicing was in complete agreement with her. The next day Robin decided to go over to Phil's barracks to ask him to go skating with her. To her surprise the first serjeant of his company was holding a little pow wow. Robin walked in the front door and in her tiny voiced asked if Phil was there. Everyone howled and yelled for Phil to come get his girl. They were still carrying on when Robin ran out in full horror. Phil took quite a bit of ribbing after that.

Robin and Phil did manage to get together the next day and Phil put on his hairpiece in the latrine. Robin stood guard at the entrance, in case anyone would venture in. The two of them went to the USO skating rink, which they were quite fond of. Robin cracked up after being hit by the same person who knocked Phil off his feet. Phil was scrambling frantically for the whereabouts of his hairpiece which had come off. He saw it laying in a dusty ball and made a dive for it, while still in the prone position. When he reached his piece he just covered it it with his whole body. Robin managed to drag Phil back to the fort hairpiece and all. When Robin had returned to her own barracks she noticed the nasty likes of corporal Pratka looking at her as she prepared to get into her bunk. He was fully aroused and didn't try to hide his feelings one bit. He had wanted her for a long time and it didn't look like he could be put off any longer. He approached her from behind. She was in her bath wrap around and he pressed himself against her behind. Robin felt the unwelcome presence and proceeded to claw it with her long nails. He gave out a loud yelp and rushed back to his bunk to recover. Robin then threw her head back and headed for the shower. Robin didn't think anvone would be in there at this late hour. Much to her surprise there was one person in the shower. It was none other than the handsome Vale. He looked at her with astonishment at first, that succumbed to a look of pure pleasure. Robin returned her look rather shyly.

He watched as she took her wrap off and turned the water on. He moved closer to her and pressed against her backside. He kissed the back of her neck and she allowed him to fondle her tiny breasts. He then kissed her full on

41

her small mouth. He rubbed his hands over her shimmering buttocks. The steam was rising and he was rising to say the least. He finally made his intrusion and she let herself be taken in wild abandonment. They held each other in the shower until almost dawn it seemed.. He told her of his undying love and that they should be together After this army stint. She said that could be a very real possibility. They were truly in the state of high bliss. Carla it seems had gone to NYC for an extended holiday. She didn't return at her appointed time and was considered awol. She was summoned into the orderly room and asked to explain her absence. She made some excuse up and fluttered her eyes at the commander. She knew he had wanted her and she knew just how to get out of this mess. He cupped her chin in his big hands and looked deeply into her exotic eyes. She had She threw her arms around him as she pulled him down to meet her tender kiss. He kissed her with a fury that left little for one to wonder what the next move would be. He picked up all 100 lbs. Of her and edged toward the door to lock it of course. He then layed her on the sofa very quietly.

Carla watched as the commander undid her tight uniform. She then busied herself with undoing his. He then pressed himself on the full length of her and took her hungrily. She clawed his back provoking all the more. They must have both climaxed at least three more times. They were stopped by the pounding at the door. He stopped his pounding to to open the door. Carla left the room in her very confident little trots. She was very pleased that he wanted to take her on an excursion to Atlanta. Robin and Carla got together that Friday after duty. Carla said that her and the gang were heading for Charlotte and the famous Blue Note lounge. Robin talked Rick into going along. Robin and Carla were waiting for the others to pick them up. They were waiting at the old division service club. They sat at their table sipping at their "colt forty fives." Carla had her hair straightened and put an auburn rinse in it. She swung her hair over one eye similiar to the style that Robin had. Robin's hair was blue black of course and she had dark brown eyes. After a short time of this, Carla heard her name being called from the upstairs balcony. It was Valucci and the very handsome Sylvester. His powder blue eyes could knock a girl over even from that distance. His hair was the purest black and with those eyes, the effect was devestating. Robin was allready tingling from the prospect of his getting near. They soon joined them at the table. Valucci sat near Carl and Sylvester near Robin. Valucci asked Carla what she was up to and she mentioned the trip to Charlotte.

Valucci said that he would like to, but he had CQ duty that night. Sylvester agreed to come along and Robin said fine. He gave Robin one of his dreamy eyed looks and she returned one of her own. He then put his hand on one of her bare legs under the table. Valucci wasted no time either and cupped a hand under Carla's squirming behind. Some one played, "Poor Side of Town," on the jukebox. The couples began to dance and they did't care who was watching. The entrance was on fire from the spectacle of Marty and Waynetta wearing the most outrageous outfits. Marty was in the lead of course, she had on what looked like a turbin. This was accompanied by a pair of very wide pantaloons. The color was a shocking purple, very bright indeed. She looked like she had just spent midnight at the oasis. Waynetta was wearing a halter affair and hot pants of french foregin legion type gauze. This number was practically see through and she wasn't about to worry what was being revealed. She let one halter strap fall, and headed over to join the others. Everyone's eyes were agape and jaws were dropping. Carla could have sworn she heard a few people choking on their food. The two queens paid them no homage and started an immediate chit chat with Carla and Robin. Marty almost blew her turbin off when she feasted her eyes on-the georgeous Sylvester. She queried Robin in loud tones with great expectency, "who is this"? Well after a moment or two the gang headed for the door and caused an after shock. Valucci said his goodbyes and went his way.The car with Samantha behnd the wheel was parked. It was a long white cadillac convertable.

Samantha's mother had bought it for her on her ninteenth birthday and she just loved it. She was wearing her hair in a gone with the wind style, complete with a fall. One wondered how long before it would be gone with the wind in this open car. They all jumped in the car and just as they did they heard a familiar scream, honeee. It was of course Mickey, and she was running full speed down the street. Her hair was not hair as anyone had seen, it it looked almost hot pink. She had on a multi colored caftan affair. She tripped when she caught the long material under one of her feet. All you could hear were her screams and all you could see was a pink and rainbow tumbleweed. She was hurtling towards the car and hit her hairdo against the front tire and collapsed in a mess. Sylvester was the only one composed enough to help the poor dear as the others were hysterical. Robin finally composed herself and helped Sylvester revive her. Robin grabbed some ice from the cooler and placed them in a handkerchief and began to pat her head. She began her wailing ooh ooh ,ah ah. They told her she could borrow something else to wear and she squeeled with delight. She had a nasty bump on her forehead. They were by this time attracting too much attention by the military, and they decided to pull out of there. Samantha hit the gas and they turned up a cloud of dust. They tore out the front gate at a hectic speed. Luckily no one was following them to give them a ticket.

They managed to escape the madness of the post and Waynetta swore someone was following them. She must have been hallucinating through her bee hive wig. Samantha's own hair was now on the side of her face. she asked Marty to fix it for her and make her look just like Scarlett Ohara. They headed out the highway for Charlotte. She wanted to be Scarlett in Charlotte. Robin and Sylvester were necking in the back seat and Mickey was swearing obcentaties from the back seat. No one could figure out whatever she was saying even if part of her Caftan was blowing in her face. Carla got her untangled from the Caftan land took it off her. She was left wearing her push up bra and red and black panties with long hooks holding up her nylons. She for some reason took out her anger on Samantha. She grabbed her by the hairpiece and part of her real hair. Samantha let out a loud scream. She let go of the wheel and made a quick lunge for Mickey. The car went off the road and ended up in a ditch. Marty was thrown onto the hood. Her turban was lying in a mud puddle. Samantha scratched Mickey and the blood on her nails blended in perfectly with her nail color. Marty salavaged her turban and put it back on her head. She began to verbally lash out at Samantha and so were the others. Waynetta had been hit in the head with the container of the water cooler and was doused with ice water. Her gauze outfit was helpless under the deluge. She had "Colt forty five's" all over her and she was babbling in her southern drawl.

Samantha hit her head, minus the Scarlett hairpiece on the dash. Mickey was thrown on the grassy bank in her push up bra and panties. She was still cussing at poor Samantha. She mixed a blend of Puerto Rican and broken English. Robin was snuggled,in the back seat with Sylvester so they were fine. The crew of them manged to settle thir differences and pull the car back onto the road. Mickey didn't even bother to dress. She simply popped open a beer and laid back. It was one of the ones Waynetta threw at her. She began singing a number from West Side Story, "Puerto Rico My hearts devotion", some one said , "please let it drop back in the ocean." They had gone along a few miles or so and came upon a bus load of football players. they were heading home from a game, one they apparently had one for their spirits were definitely up. They saw the queens and the queens saw them. It was instant madness. The guys were screaming and the queens who were allready screaming were screaming some more. Some guy held an athletic supporter out the window. They loved this and were reaching to grab it. Marty and Waynetta were trying to get it by standing up in the back seat of the car. Marty caught one over her head and some guys had their appendages hangin out in full view. Waynetta and Marty had their hands and mouths open to catch a prize. Marty had one guy by his member and how she managed to keep up the rythum was amazing. Robin was totally shocked by her brazen behavior. She wanted no part of this madness. Samantha could hardly keep her one hand on the wheel. She was tring to grab waving members with the other one.

This went on for twenty miles or so and the bus had to take a different road so the queens screamed their goodbyes and the boys yelled theirs. The girls speeded up and were very anxious to get to Charlotte and the bar. Before they had gone too much further they heard sirens and saw much to their dismay, a police car approaching. Samantha had second thoughts about trying to lose them. She decided the effort would be futile and pulled the car over to await this most unwelcome event. Two big and burly numbers got out of the patrol car. They didn't seem too friendly either. One grabbed a shocked Marty by the head turbin and all. He placed his other hand on her skinny butt and proceede to yank her out of the car. She began to wail as he put her down and demanded to see her id. He looked at the ID and then at her and wanted to know why the child didn't have female instead of male on it. She replied "darling " you know how that goes." He said he didn't and slapped a pair of handcuffs on her skinny wrists. Waynetta protested and he slapped another pair on her. They figured they had a handfull with the two of them, so they left the others and headed of for the Bugbern jail. Marty kicked one to the officers when he cupped a hand over her skinny behind. Waynetta was furiosly groping the other one, hoping of course to be let go. Samantha and the others were following close behind in the car. Samantha was shouting obcentaties in her southern drawl. They arrived at the jail and threw the two girls in a cell with some drunken men.

Waynetta managed to get a call off to her ill tempered mother in Fayetteville. She wailed into the phone "Maw "I'm here in Bugern, in this god awfull jail". Her mother replied into the phone, "you quarr whoring sumna bitch," "when I get my hands on you, " "I'll give you a sex change" She asked to speak to the sheriff and explained thet her brother was a judge in that county and that they better let them go if they didn't want trouble from him. That was enough for the sheriff, and he let the poor girls go. Marty was shaking so much her turban nearly fell off again.

Waynetta started getting wobbly kneed. Marty grabbed her by the skinny wrist and went outside to meet the others. Samantha gave Marty and Waynetta a beer to calm them down. Mickey said they should be more careful in flawless puerto rican and then english. Marty straightened her turbin on her shaken head and Waynetta adjusted her halter. She tried to make her breasts push up larger even though they were the size of crabapples. She just had to start taking more pills. She was afraid her mother would find them in one of her many raids she pulled on her room. One night she came bursting in at midnight, waking Waynetta out of a dreamy sleep. She claimed she had smelled marijuanna coming from the room. She demanded a shakedown and didn't care how late it was. Waynetta threw an alarm clock at her and the woman nearly threw the child out of the second floor window.

Marty and Mickey were now lighting up joints and started to giggle almost instantly. The burning ash from the joint somehow ended up in Mickey's hairy armpit and you could smell the burnig hair and deodorant. You could also hear rather audible screams coming from the poor dear. Marty reprimanded Mickey for not shaving. Mickey replied that in Puerto Rico it was not the custom to do so. They finally reached the Charlotte city limits and they headed straight for the Blue Note. When they arrived at the bar it was packed. It must have been somebody's birthday because they were carrying on more than usual. Someone grabbed Marty's turban and she grabbed his privates. She refused to let go after he had returned her turban. She squeezed harder and he bit her long nipples. They ended up on the dance floor doing a wild jitterbug. Her pantaloons were positively flaring out. Mickey grabbed some poor boy and tried to outdo Marty in a wild spanish style number.

The poor boy was helpless to try and follow this child. Robin and Sylvester began to dance very slow and very close. He kissed her full on the mouth and she laad her head on his broad shoulder. This one queen with an outfit that consisted of a mini skirt and conchita top with high white boots, moved in on Mickey's partner. Mickey was more patient than usual and then finally blew it and made a lunge for the queen's conchita top. The queen called, Decima, fought back and had Mickey in a headlock. She then put a cigarette lighter to Mickeys frizzy hairdo and threatened to light it on fire.

Mickey didn't relent and the queen lit the hairdo and Mickey with smoldering hair and all charged the crowd like a wounded bull. The crowd managed to douse the hair with a mixture of their exotic drinks. She made it to the ladies room with lemon and lime peels in her frazzeled hair. Lucky for her their wasn't too much damage done and she managed to comb out most of the burned parts. She returned from all of this to find her friend dancing with Decima. He was holdinq her close with one hand down her conchita top. Mickey then walked over and gave her a high kick on her high rump. Decima retaliated by giving Mickey a spiking with her high heels, in a most unforgiveable area. Mickey was on the floor and people thought she was demonstrating a new dance. Mickey managed to throw her handbag from an awkward position with all of its heavy contents at Decima. The makeup scattered everywhere, Maybelline, Revlon, Cover Girl,and a few items from Max Factor. The crowd helped her retrieve her precious cargo and she thanked them in two languages. The party atmosphere was heavy in the air. The manager told everyone to make way for the band. They were of course a queen's band and they of course expected to be treated just like royalty. The leader of the troupe was called Seance, and she had an explosion of frizzy blonde hair. Her hair looked like it weighed more than her whole skinny body. She had a body that resembled a pick up stick. They were called the pick up sticks aptly. They started to play and pick their instruments with their long purple nails. They started with a number called, "Double Shot of My Baby's Love".

All you could see from the far end of the bar were bony knees, and rumps kicked upby spiked heeled go go boots, that looked high enough to engulf them in. This was all in the glare of the psychedelic light. Carla got so carried away that she ran up to the stage and asked them for the mike so she could do a number. She sang, "Dancing In The Street". Everyone went wild applauding and dancing. She started into "Heat Wave", and everyone went wild. Robin went up and joined her and proceeded to do a solo. She chose the number, "Coming on Strong" She then followed up with, "Love is Here and Now You Are Gone". They both dueted in, "you Keep Me Hanging On". The pick up sticks were anxious to get back to center stage and Robin and Carla exited with much fanfare. Carla ran to the phone to call Vallucci and Robin ran to Sylvester's waiting arms. Mickey had made up with Decima and they were doing the Hullaballo on the dance floor. Mickey was wearing one of Waynetta's Sheena Queen of the Jungle, tops hanging over one shoulder. She complimented this with a plastic nearly see through, mini shirt. She had on a pair of roman sandals. She did Mickey's own style of monkey to the song of the same name. The band was really picking up on this number and by this time they were feeling no pain. After a few more numbers the police arrived and had everyone line up against the wall. They said they were looking for a few

50

hookers, who worked the area around the Blue Note. They went after their first suspect, Mickey.

Mickey of course was beside herself with anger and began to spill out obcentities in her native tongue. She managed to calm herself down enough to tell them that she was in the army at Ft Bragg. They of course, laughed in her face, until she produced her military ID. She had it stuffed in her very un military undergarment. They questioned her about her true hair color. She told them it was none of their business in broken english. They just laughed and went on to check some of the others out. They spotted Marty and went promply over to her. She asked them if they had ever heard of the Yon Baker's of Germany. She made no bones about her royal lines. She was left alone after producing her driver's licence. She was just about to explain her family jewels when they walked away. The Pick up Sticks were now swearing at the police about disrupting their performance. They didn't have long to wait after they had stopped playing. The police left and the band played "Sunny". Everyone started to get sunny again. This madness went on for a few more hours and someone got up on the stage to announce an after hours party. So when the bar closed about a hundred and fifty sreaming queens marched down the street to their party site. They made so much noise people were looking out of their windows. They dropped a few jaws and some nearly fell out of their windows to gawk at them. They knew the flag day parade didn't start until noon. They arrived at the house where the party was to be held.

How they ever managed to get into that house was left to the explanation. The owner of the place was a black drag queen called "Ursula~ She even had the bartender from the club working her bar fixing drinks. Everyone was delighted with this arrangement and on the upstairs balcony the band set up. Their first number was "Papa's got a Brand New Bag". Ursula's mother began to do a wild dance to this and everyone cheered her on. Marty then joined in and it did't take Mickey long to follow. Carla had become preoccupied with a sailor who popped in from Wilmington. She led him to the dance floor with her jutting behind as bait. She looked like a bitch in heat to say the least. She started to undulate to the music and he had his mouth hanging open. she looked at him invitingly and urged him to her provacatively: He pulled her into his vice grip and she didn't struggle. Marty had taken up with a fat boy who had his fat hands all over her skinny body. She just glowed with fever in her bloodshot eyes. She threw a skinny arm around his spare tire as they danced. Mickey of course was holding court at the bar area. She was instructing the bartender on the latest Carribean drinks. She just squeeled with delight at some one complimenting her on one of her creations. Ursula was gathering reqruits for a chorus line on the balcony. She picked Robin and Carl out to do the can can. The pick up sticks accompanied them with "Uptight" the crowd was rolling on that number. As this was going on, ten marines came in the front door and joined the party to no ones dismay.

The marines instantly ran up to the balcony to join in on the can can. Robin, Carla, and Ursula were now really whipped up and danced in a near frenzy. The boys threw them over their heads and did other variations. Carla was thrown over the balcony and managed to escape injury by being caught by some hunk. Two of the marines held Ursula outstretched and tossed her nearly to the ceiling. Robin was flanked by two numbers who each held her hand

and did the high kick with her. Marty, Mickey, and Waynetta raced up the stairs to each grab a man and join in the fun. The house rocked so hard you'd swear they were in the middle of an earthquake. The Pick Up Sticks were rocking from another balcony and they started to play "The Stripper". Waynetta and Carla started to disrobe and soon the others followed. They were throwing various items of clothing and jewelery down on the people in the living room. Someone got a Von Baker necklace in his drink. Someone else was hit with the turban. Carla threw her undies in her sailor friend's face. They were giving the people downstairs moonshots in unision. The late arrival marines began to undress. Uniforms,iockstaps, medals, and other items of clothing were raining down. Without too much time the people downstairs started to get into the act. Pretty soon nearly everone was buck naked. It looked like a nudist dance. After a few more moments of this someone heard a knock on the front door.

It turned out to be their next door neighbor. She was middle aged and dressed in a frumpy house dress. She entered the place and demanded to know what was going on. She got the picture in about five blinks of her eyes. Her eyes got locked onto the balcony area where the nude can can was being performed. Mickey screamed "oh honey", to her and gave her a full moon shot. The lady jusk gawked at the wonder of it. She then demanded to know the whereabouts of Ursula. Someone grabbed her in an embrace and she suddenly forgot what she came in for. She listened to the music and began to dance. The next thing you know she began to undress. She took off her jumbo bra and the rest of her large garments. Someone began to dance with her and she let her self go completely. She ground her self out of her huge panties and continued to dance. She threw her panties up to the second floor. She let go a primitive scream and grabbed a dance partner. Carla was pinned up against the balcony by a huge man. She could barely do her proper dance motions. Mickey was being violated by someone and making strange noises in two languages. Marty was caked in oil and looked like she didn't have much spunk left in her. Waynetta was swinging on a chandelier and jumping in to someone's arms in a most provocative way. There was a knock at the door and Marcetto and Horn had entered. How they got here was anybody's guess.

Marcetto started dancing her solo number singing her own song to accompany herself. Of course it was a Streisand number. The frumpy housewife was being lifted by some strong men and tossed into a sea of dancers. She was laughing hysterically. The pick up sticks had thrown all of their clothes into the crowd. Their skinny butts and lemon sized breasts were shaking to the beat. One band member had hair down to her butt and was singing a Cher number. One of the other members was singing like Sonny to accompany her on one of their big hits. Marty was not to be seen, but you could hear her babbling from a pile of greased bodies. Carla was cleaning out her ear and someone put something into the other one. Waynetta was hanging from a rafter and two guys were trying to pull her down. The housewife was in an orgasmic state after someone brought her to full flower. Where in the world was her husband? She was mumbling someones name under what ever breathe she had left. Robin and Sylvester had gone into one of the bedrooms and were locked into each others arms. Marcetto was still twirling but she had attracted some man to her and he was trying to follow her in her mad dance. They had sex and her expression hadn't changed. Marty had struggled from the pile of bodies and wanted a drink. Carla was being torn apart by two men fighting over her. She of course was determined to have both of them. The fat lady was slithering down the stairs after having been bombarded with unholy approaches. Mickey was trying to get to the bar to play bartender.

Mickey was trying to get to the bar also, she had her fill of seaman and semen. Marty and Mickey converged on the bar area and Mickey followed. She promptly ordered a Kamchatka vodka stinger. Marty ordered a salty margarita, to match her salty tongue. Waynetta finally gave up her trapeze act after failing to climax that way. She managed to achieve it more than once, and with more than one partner, the conventional way. If you can call anything that that queen does conventional. She got up from one pile of bodies and dived in another one afterwards. Her hair was matted and greasy looking but her vanity had gone out the window or some other way, several hours ago. Carla was now doing a dance with a feather boa and two sailors, all very South Pacific style. She was touching them in very strange places while she did her sleazy dance. Robin and Sylvester had fallen asleep in each other's arms. The fat lady had been abused by every kind of sadistic treatment. She managed to achieve a few orgasms through all the roughness. The band had been assaulted by some other commandoes. One of them was in a harness and some fool was having his way with her. Mickey charged up the stairs and threatened to play an instrument if the "pick up sticks" didn't pick up playing. Marty was right behind her and her behind was beginning to sag a little from all the stress put upon it. Mickey didn't even bother to find her revlon cream to massage her red areas. Ursula came out of the kitchen with some overdue snacks. The fat lady was the first to thank her.

After stuffing her face the fat lady went up the stairs to ask the band to let her do a number. The band gave her a mike and she did an old number called, "I need it ". The band picked up the beat and she managed to get through it and so did the audience. She hit some strange notes when someone tried intercourse from behind. The audience finally bombarded her from the stage. She cursed them out for what it was worth. It was now getting close to dawn and the party was starting to thin out. People were getting dressed and heading for the door. Carla went into one of the bedrooms and was joined by two sailor admirers who quickly made a place for her on the floor. She was now in a beautiful sandwich and and didn't care how she was to be consumed. Robin walked in and observed a blissful look on her brown little face. Mickey, Marty, and Waynetta had set up sleeping areas in the living room. They each had a man to keep them warm and comfy on the floor. The band had fallen asleep next to their instruments and Ursula locked up and proceeded to the master bedroom. She had a cute number with her to keep her company. The fat lady had long ago put on her house dress and gone home to her hubby. When it got to be noon the queens decided to go on to Wilmington before heading back to Fayetteville. Wilmington was on the coast and had a kicky little bar that the sailors liked to frequent. When they arrived at the bar they immediately made themselves at home. Carla took up with a sailor and he took her up in his huge arms.

Robin accepted a dance with another big guy. He looked down at her with pure admiration and a little more arousal. Robin liked the way he looked at her. Waynetta danced with Marty who had a scarf around her head and did a belly dance. Some queens were laughing at her and Marty lold them to watch it. One queen got to be too much for Marty's nerves and she let the queen have it accross the face with her scarf. The drink she had was knocked over in the process. Some of it had spilled onto her yellow jumpsuit and it was now pink in spots. She had been drinking sloe gin. She was fit to be tied and raced over to Marty and tried to tie her up with her own scarf. Marty couldn't believe how strong the queen was. She had tied Marty's wrists and ankles together and curled her up into what looked like a skinny bony ball. Then she gave Marty a hard slap accross the cheek and grabbed her man and walked out. Mickey became hysterical and Waynetta joined her in the laughter. Carla went over to Miss Baker and untied the poor child. Carla saw the anger in Marty's face and had to stifle a snicker to avoid her wrath. Marty jumped up and bolted toward the door looking out in vain for the queen. Mickey bought her a brandy alexander and tried to soothe her by asking questions about her Von Baker heritage. That of course did the trick. Waynetta found herself a trick and danced up a storm with him. She had on low cut huggers with a jewelf shining out from her skinny navel. Her jeans flared out into elephant bells as she flared out onto the dancing floor.

Her pants were black and dotted with scores of rhinestones of various colors. Her top was vinyl with provacative cut outs. Her butt was twizzling to the Beach Boys rendition of "I get Around ". Her dance partner got a hand on that real quick. Marty was now smoking out of a near foot long cigarette holder, while conversing with a severely made up Mickey. Her cover girl was overworked today and that shade of purple lipstick was about to do in her Puerto Rican lips. She might even get thrown out of the bar for being too much for anyone's eyes. Marty's tube top was bad enough especially with that Svengali scarf. She was wearing the highest go go boots along with the highest mini skirt. Her tutu played peek a boo in it. Carla was wearing her skin tight doeskin pants along with a white ruffled blouse. Under neath she sported a Frederick's push up bra. Robin had on leather hot pants with a gold lame sleeveless metallic top. Her hair was quite fetching with the blue black fall she had attached. She had no need for nylons with her beautifully tanned legs. Her dancing partner took notice of how soft they were to the touch. After this the girls decided to call one of their friends who had a beach house. They were invited over for a get together. They brought along some of the guys they had been dancing with and jumped in several cars. Samantha was behind the wheel of her car and had been sleeping in it while everyone was in the bar.

That girl could sleep as much as Carla, who sometimes slept sixteen hours a day. They drove on through Wilmington and finally arrived at the house of their friend. Samantha adjusted her Gone with the Wind wig and Marty threw her skinny scarf around her equally skinny neck. Carla adjusted her pants and Robin did the same to her hot ones. Their friend Pam came to the door and greeted the girls. Mickey and Waynetta lead the way with the men in tow. Pam's mother looked on with a shocked look on her face. She decided to go to her room rather than be a part of this circus. Robin and Samantha discussed Samantha's friend Teacher and what a chicken plucker that one was. He was supposed to be in town for the weekend and they figured he went imediately to the YMCA. They called over there and sure enough he was there. They invited him over and he arrived with a sixteen year old. Teacher was just besides himself for having snagged this chicken. Teacher wanted him to come back and live with him in Fayetteville. The boy was estranged from his family and of course said yes. Mickey squeeled, "Teacher honee ", when she saw him. She went over and started the bar up. Marty was fooling with the stereo and Robin was out in the kitchen making up some spaghetti. Mickey soon had everyone supplied with a drink as they begin to settle in. Robin had a Mai Tai while she was cooking and Marty had herself a grasshoopper. Waynetta demanded a sloe gin fizz. Mickey made herself a rum and coke. Waynetta was entertaining one of the guys they brought along. She was sitting in her very super close manner. Her long dangling legs were crossed and she was flaunting herself to the fullest. Her hair was very Veronica Lake hanging over one eye. She spoke of her relationship with her mother. She put her seductive radar on hold while she became emotional over her mother's treatment of her. She spoke of another incident involving her staff sergeant boy friend. Her mother it seemed had found them together and at a critical moment. She was just about to throw her long legs over the man's shoulders. Her mother burst in and let out a squirk similiar to that of a bunch of hens. The serjeant jumped up with a full erection in full view of her mother. The poor woman nearly fell unconscious. Waynetta told her in very loud terms to get the hell out. Her mother recovered enough to scream out her famous quarrs, quarrs !! She said that she was going to have the minister exorcize Waynetta. Waynetta threw one of her spiked heels at her mother, and she and the man fled to the Prince Charles hotel to continue. Waynetta resumed her seducing act after relating this flash back to her present partner. Mickey was jumping up a down on some one's lap and squeeling in her usual high pitched manner. Marty was discussing her family tree, what else. She said they even had a family crest and that there were dukes and dutchesses in her lineage. She continued on about the castles they lived in and how they had many servants catering to their needs. She spoke of her estate in Fayetteville and her help. Robin and Carla heard this and wanted to yell for help at this blasphamy.

Marty kept on weaving her fabrication without a moments pause. She went on how her upstairs maid couldn't get along with her downstairs one. Her butler she said with conviction, couldn't keep his hands from her body. She said one day in her limo, he locked her in and jumped her in the back seat. He forced her to have oral sex and she was too overwhelmed to resist. She went on how she almost lost her voice afterwards. Her voice did sound rather squeeky. Robin went into the kitchen and brought out her fabulous spaghetti. Everyone was starved and had more than one helping. One hunk grabbed Robin and told her she could cook for him anytime. She said that she would love to. Carla said to anyone who would listen, that no one could top her cornbread. Mickey said that she could throw together a puerto rican loaf, that only she could whip up. Marty of course had to mention her German strudel. It was starting to get dark and more people had arrived. Thre queens and five marines were at the front door. The queens turned out to be the band, The Pick Up Sticks, and they had their instruments with them ready to play. Everyone screamed when they saw them. The crowd recovered from last night and were ready to rock and roll again. Pam told the band where to set up and a squeeling Mickey led the marines to the bar area. She sat them down and started to touch them in forbidden areas. She wanted to go further but they said that they were thirsty. She replied that her throat was dry also. They laughed and ordered what they wanted. Carla told her to hurry with her cream and sherry soda.

Sylvester was talking about staying in the army for twenty years. He asked Robin if she would do also. Carla said that she was going to help move her family to LA when she got leave. She talked of going there after her enlistment was up. The band began to play "When a Man Loves a Woman ", and a blond and burly marine caught Robin's hand and led her to the dance floor. Carla went over to the bar area and picked out a red head and began to dance with him. She was about to explode in the rear of her doeskin pants as she undulated. She wouldn't let up and give the material some relief. She started in with an evil bump and grind. Then she started using her beau as a conveyor belt for her grinding butt. The crowd stopped dancing and began to watch her. Thank God there were drapes to wrap herself in if necessary. Marty joined in and did grab the drapes in her Bagdad seven veils dance. Waynetta thought she was going to get dramatic and pull her wrist slicing act again. She loved it when she had the audience spellbound. This time of course was no exception. Her doctors had always told her that she was a frustrated star. She even starred in a few things in the Fayetteville playhouse. Her favorite role was that of Blanche DuBois in Streetcar. They had offered her the Marlon Brando part and she told them who she was. She did, "The Boys in The Band". Her mother brought some of her queen bee friends to see that one. Marty was disturbed from the noise in the audience and threw an ash tray from the set.

The ash tray nearly knocked her mother's wide brim hat off. People in the audience began pelting Marty with various items and she was throwing things back. The scene had gotten totally out of control and Marty had to crawl on all fours backstage to escape. She as a result , was almost thrown out of the play. Back at the party Marty urged the others to resume dancing after she had exhausted herself. She threw her scarf aroung her partner and dragged him to the sofa. She pulled out her long cigarette holder and placed a Raleigh king in it and took a long draw. Her cigarette holder was covered in jewels. She explained how she normally only smoked imported German cigarettes. She said she was waiting in a new shipment. Mickey came over with two drinks and offered one to Marty and she thanked her in German. Mickey acknowledged in Spanish. Carla was pooped after her exhibition on the dance floor and threw her self and her man on the other end of the sofa.She was telling the guy how she used to pick cotton in Mississippi. Marty was absolutely appalled at this. She said she would never get near a cotton field let alone work in one. She asked Carla if she was just doing this for amusement. Carla replied in all honesty that she needed the money it brought in. Carla also mentioned how a black stud threw her over a cotton bale in an initiation process. She said that night she had to pick more cotton out of her hair. She mentioned how she had a crush on some one at high school and had written him a note. One day after school he followed her and they went into the woods.

Carla went on to say that he took advantage of her against her wishes. She explained that she said to him can't we just wait. Mickey smiled and said, "wait for what? The showboat for New Orleans." Carla said that at the time she would have loved to have performed on a showboat, but the Mississippi river didn't run through Clarksdale. Robin brought up the relating topic of a boy she had known when she was in high school. He had been like a boyfriend to her and they used to go to the movies together. He would pretend to be asleep and reach for her hand and touch her foot with his. He also liked to get on top of her when they crashed in the sled riding trains they were involved with. They had a fight one day and Robin's german shepherd dog bit into his butt. He made a big fuss about it. Mickey then of course had to tell everyone about her affair. She had known this boy in Puerto Rico named Alfredo. He lived near her on the outskirts of San Juan. They lived in the same apartment complex. One day Mickey was in the laundry room doing her laundry and Alfredo walked in. He knew Mickey was a hot little queen and she wasn't used to using the word no, when it came to sex. He locked the door behind him and then locked on to her behind. He promised to take Mickey to the school prom in full drag. Pam came down the stairs as Mickey was finishing up her little story.

She was accompanied by teacher and his little teenage trick. Pam knew Teacher from the bar he had made many trips to Wilmington on his chicken hunts. He asked Mickey about some of the young Puerto Rican chicken. Mickey replied that it was brown and quite appetizing. Marty said that she preferred Kentucky fried. Waynetta said that she had always wanted to try Yankee roosters. Marty asked Robin if she had tried Quaker and Robin thought she must be kidding. Pam suggested that they go out onto the patio and look at the sunset. The sun was going down in a blaze over the water. The girls decided to change into their bathing suits. It was ironic that they packed them for this trip. Marty put on her very skimpy zebra suit. This number barely covered her crab apple breasts. Her skinny behind was another story. Waynetta had a skinny black suit that looked almost topless. It was cut low in the back and had criss cross straps on the back. Her thighs were exposed to the waist before anyone had ever thought of doing it. Robin put on her Miss Universe number. It was cut very low in front almost to the waist. One sailor had to reach for her appealing breasts. She slapped his hand and he just laughed and grabbed her up in his arms and raced for the water. Carla was in sheer black nylon and silk. This number was a Fredrick's exclusive. The suit looked like hot pants with suspenders. She ran into the water with her brown nipples leading the way.

Two hungry men were following her close behind. She treated them with her usual cool indifference. They raced to get to her in the water. It was one of those Atlantic sunsets and the water was purple and orange. Carla later lay on the beach Cleo style and gave the two men curious Looks as one of them tried to rearrange her suit. Her bouncing buttocks quivered to his touch. He began to kiss and caress her pointed nipples. She merely lit a cigarette and looked at him with amused boredom. The other one was kissing her neck. She turned and gave him one of her famous, I don't give a dam looks. Mickey and Waynetta were in the water on the shoulders of two hunks. Marty was caught in a wave out further, and her suit was askew. Her hair was all stringy over her panic stricken eyes. The waves brought her in tumbles on her favorite position all fours. Waynetta and Mickey were knocked off the shoulders of the two guys and were nearly knocked unconscious. Mickey had a crab biting her behind and she screamed for any honey. Waynetta had seaweed creating a new hairdo for her while she was rammed into the beach agianst some driftwood. Robin looked like she was body surfing when she rode in. Carla had her cigarette put out and her bathing suit nearly taken out to sea by a huge wave. She never dreamed it would come in and strike her. That didn't stop her from instantly lighting up another one. Her brown nipples had turned pink, like they had been sandpapered. She of course couldn't even be bothered. She had the two men attending her like slaves.

Looking out from the beach, Marty was being brought in by Mickey and Waynetta. The looked like they needed bringing in themselves. Pam ran out with fresh drinks to revive the victims. Marty was choking on sand and seaweed, but she asked for a double scotch. After everyone had recovered a bit the men built a fire on the beach and began to roast weenies and marshmellows. Everyone gathered around the fire and Robin sang a number acompanied by the band. Carla did another one after Robin did hers. Someone was bending their stck to get the marshmellow from it flew off and hit Marty, almost burning her lipstick off. She wanted to prong another one into whoever did it. She started talking to herself in German. She couldn't take much more. She got up in the ruins of her suit and headed for the water again. She wanted to wash her lipstick and she prayed another wave wouldn't do her in. Carla was looking across the fire at Waynetta's man. He reminded her so much of her precious Valucci. She was giving him her Sheba look beckoning and seductive. He started to look back at Carla and Waynetta said something to him. He was not responding to her as he was caught up in Carl's spell. Waynetta had to grab him and practically shake him out of it. She then glared over at Carla. Carla gave her one of her best, I don't give a dam looks. Waynetta by now started to sizzle and she picked up a sizzling stick and threw it at Carla. Carla just laughed as it went sailing by. Waynetta then got up and ran over to Carla and grabbed for her hair.

Carla then proceeded to bite into one of Waynetta's skinny nipples. Waynetta then screamed and in her best southern drawl, called Carla a black bitch, noting that he was her man!!. Carla said that she didn't even know what the girl could possibly be referring to. She lit another cigarette and slowly and deliberately gave the man another provocotive look. Waynetta was so shook up by this that her skinny legs wobbled severely. She ran up to the house in a nervous twitter. The man moved overto where Carla was and acted as if Waynetta didn't even exist. Carla looked at him in bored amusement and said , oh so matter of factly, "how are you" ? He responded by taking her in his huge arms and asking her, "where have you been"? She replied, "I thought you'd never ask". Waynetta came out of the house and threw her head back haughtily, as she sat down beside another man. Carla of course couldn't even be bothered. She took out another one of her longest cigarettes and motioned for the man to light it. She blew the smoke Waynetta's direction. Casually, Marcetto twirled out of the house in a normal stupor state and was of course involved with herself, singing another Streisand number. Someone laughed at her very loudly and said thet she needed another blow on the head to bring her back. A man then ran up to her and grabbed her, and began to dance with her. Marcetto barely acknowledged his prescence and laughed and talked to no one in particular.

As he was spinning her around she was making grand gestures, while singing the number "people", very loudly. He squeezed her too hard and she hit a high note. Everyone began to dance put on their own little shows. Carla was persuaded up from the sand with Waynetta's ex, who happened to be an ex ex, as he was Samanthas partner when the party began. Robin and Sylvester were locked tightly in each others arms. Marty and some number were doing what could only be described, as the sand shuffle. Mickey had a grasshopper in her hand and she and a big marine were doing their version of the dance. Mickey looked very small in comparison to the man. This madness carried on past midnight and after that they all had to get back to the post. Our soldier girls had to be at their duty stations at seven thirty sharp. Waynetta refused to sit next to or to speak to Carla in the car. Carla raised a tiny eyelid her way. Robin and Slyvester were again involved in the back seat. Mickey, Waynetta nad Samantha were in the front seat and Marty squeezed in beside Robin and Sylvester in the back seat. Marty put her famous turban on again and she had the matching pantalooms on and they were so wide they seemed to take up extra space. Samanthas driving hadn't changed any she was doing at least eighty with the top down destroying everyone's hairdos. Well at least Marty had her's conditioned with sea weed and kelp. She of course took the turban off when Samantha hit the gas for the first time.

Samantha wasn't in the least concerned with people's hairdo's as she fancied herself a driver on the order of Shirley Muldooney. Marty's long cigarette holder was rendered useless in this draft. She might as well knock out her nicotine fit with a can of copenhagen. Sylvester had just offered her some and she took a wad and stuck it in her skinny cheek. She said in her high pitched squeel, that it wasn't half bad. The trouble began when she had to spit out, and Samantha caught a squirt in her heavily mascarad eyeball. The car careened across the white line, completely out of control, nearly hitting a semi head on. Samantha somehow managed to regain control, but not before everone was on top of everyone else. Mickey and Waynetta were fighting in the front seat after Waynetta's long bony elbow boned Mickey's ear, tearing off her long studded earring in the process. Mickey grabbed Waynetta's skinny neck right under her adam's apple, as it was it looked like it was about to pop. Waynetta was already in a bad mood over Carla's previous antics. She wasn't about to start taking it from Mickey now. She retaliated by pushing her palm in Mickey's big mouth, crushing her big spanish lips. Mickey then screamed that Waynetta had gotten lipstick all over her pretty white teeth. Waynetta responded that she would soon have it all over her face. Waynetta then turned around and asked Carla if she wanted any more trouble. Carla just laughed her tiny little laughs and asked Waynetta to please watch her southern temper.

"Who did she think she was anyway", "Scarlett OHara'!? Waynetta just snickered, "Yew beetch" in her fullest southern drawl. Marty's face was covered in snuff juices and her turban was unrecognizeable under Sylvester's big boot. She was about to give him a boot when he wasn't looking but Robin put a stop to that. Sylvester saw Marty's face and asked if she would like another wad of snuff. They arrived futelly and very finally in the truck stop area of Fayetteville's suburbs. Marry said of course, that she'd like to stop and look around. They parked in a far corner of the truck stop, next to two big rigs. Marty had seen her first prospect already, and was hell bent on landing this shark. Samantha, Mickey and Marty were like hunters who had picked up the scent of a kill. The other two were already out of the car to join Marty on the hunt. Waynetta went up to one rig with her famous walk. "Hi she said","I'm from around these here parts, where are you all from"? The man answered that he was from Iowa and told her what else he wanted. Waynetta gave him her best Scarlett 0 'Hara look, and said "Gosh almighty I don't do that in the first five minutes. She then asked him if he liked to kisss, and he replied that he didn't kiss boys. Waynetta drew back and said that she was no boy and that she was a queen, she went on to explain that she was more woman than his wife. He had to agree that he found her very feminine and then he proceeded to throw a lip lock on her.

She couldn't get a breath, and he wouldn't release his seal around her mouth and bruised lips. When he finally released her from .his powerful grip, she gasped, "Oh my, you are strong aren't you?" He blushed and said that , "yes he was". She then tugged at the curly~ furry tuffs of hair on his massive chest. He developed an enormous erection and she readied herself for this big intruder. She locked her long legs around his broad shoulders and received his manhood. She never felt so exquisite after her initial scream. They began to pick up steam and they were really smoking. Waynetta began to develop a cramp in her calf from so much leg work. The trucker was grunting and making very loud other sounds and these brought on her final climatic thrust, almost sending her through the roof of the truck. Carla was in the state of occupado in another truck. She was involved with a big blonde burly number. She was being very gratefully consumed by him and he was well endowed. She fit neatly into his truck bunk and he managed to fit nicely into her. Her cleo claws dug into his well muscled back. This excited him all the more and drove into her repeatedly. She moaned in her so called Egyptian fashion, giving vent to her boiling blood. She thought and acted as if she were Nefertitti reincarnated. The trucker couldn't argue with her as he gave vent to his load of love potion. Carla felt it charge up her anxious canal. He then kissed her tiny lips and held her tiny form in his big one.

He asked Carla to come to Colorado with him but she had duty the next day. She invited him over to the house that they all had rented off post. Robin left a sleeping Sylvester and decided to see what was going on with the others. Robin was interupted by a burly hunk, he had her favorite shade of blonde hair and blue eyes. He favored Robert Redford only more on the burly side. He took in her full figure with her long tanned legs. He then began to stroke her legs with a lot of ardor. Robin didn't want to get involved but let her self go after he enveloped her with his hot kisses. He remarked how soft her skin was and he pulled her to him once again. He then picked her up like she weighed next to nothing and placed her in his sleeping area. His truck bed was never so inviting. He slowly took away her silk tank top and shorts. He kissed her up and down and put her hand on his excitement. She was in a high state of seduction with a look of dazed bliss on her pretty face. He kissed her rosebud nipples near to perfection while gently squeezing her breasts. She hung her long legs on his broad shoulders and he drove into her sweet behind. He was very gentle at first but then progressed to urgent thrusts. He kissed her and enveloped her with his horse power like a true stallion. He told her he wanted to see more of her and she liked that. She invited him to the house for a few days.

Marty and Mickey and Waynetta were all three running down the rest area heading for the woods. They were screaming full throttle and were in a furious run to lose the vice officers that were in pursuit of them. Before she knew what hit her Marty caught a blackjack on the back of her

70

head. This sent her sprawling into the bushes. She landed in a grotesque position looking very dishsheveled. Mickey and Waynetta were trying to climb the barbed wire fence. They were grabbed by two of the men as they were nearly over the top. The queens were asked by the officers what were they doing here and they replied that they were resting up from a road trip. They went on that they were stretching their legs before getting some sleep. The men thought that they were stretching their story but let them go after checking their identification. Samantha was detained in a truck with a bear of a man. He was growling while he explored her delights much to her delight. She of course invited him to the house also. They all left the truck stop in a huge convoy to the house for further fun. The queens were beside themselves with joy at the outcome of this adventure. The sun could be seen in the distance making its first advance on the horizon.

Carla and Robin and Mickey had to kiss and run as soon as they arrived at the house. They had duty today and had to be there or else. They promised everyone they would be there right after they were done with their day's work. Robin arrived at her barracks first due to the proximity to the Fayetteville highway to her area. She rushed to her locker to change into her skintight uniform. She had to first take off her makeup in the latrine. She did this to the watchful eve of Marcus, the hatefull jealous closet Queen. Marcus couldn't resist remarking."I know that you didn't just get in off C.0.. Robin replied. "not Quite honey". "Where ever I was was a lot better than being here, watching Your feeble attempts at getting close to the boys" Marcus made like he was going to throw something at Robin, who merely threw her head back and laughed. Robin made it back to the office just as they were letting in the first recuits to be Processed. she began interviewing a hunk from Atlanta , who said that he was a D.J. · before being drafted. Robin reached for the folder and he reached for her hand. She let her hand rest in his before going on with her typing, He looked deeply into her eyes, which were fluttering slightly. He asked where she was staying and she gave him directions. He managed to squeeze her hand one last time. Carla was just getting to work at the 26th Artillary and she had plenty of her own to give them if they gave her any flak today.

The first shirt just gave her one of his, I hate you so looks. Carla merely fluttered her tiny eyelids at him and rearranged her butt on her chair and begin typing She couldn't even be bothered with the likes of him today. Carla sat there typing and dreaming of the big hunk waiting for her at the house. Mickey, meanwhile almost knocked over her locker with at least a hundred cosmetics in her rush to get dressed. It was eight o'clock and her troops were in bed. They were supposed to be at the training site at seven thirty. She was in such a frenzy she forgot to take off her false eyelashes. They were long and rather obvious, but then everything about her was obvious. She didn't put forth much of an effort to hide anything either. Neither did her best friends Tina and Rosemary, for that matter. She was another Puerto Rican queen from of all places Queens. She had just gotten off the boat caught her breathe and was drafted. She didn't even have time to put on her best face. She and her friends made numerous makeup runs to Fayetteville and sometimes as far as Charlotte. They had to have the latest line of everything from Max Factor to Merle Norman. Mickey got into her version of the tight uniform and proceeded to the bay area and began screaming loud enough to rattle the windows. She rattled her troops to say the least. "You mothers had better geet up get dressed right now"!!

"You better be ready to roll in five minutes"!! She began hitting the bed rails with her teachers stick. She jerked one man to attention by the genitiles and he promptly rose to the occasion. She was double timing them to get them in a hurry to the training site. When they finally arrived at the site, the Staff serjeant in charge, pulled back and roared at her like an overwrought lion. Mickey just looked at him defiently, with her Puerto Rican blood beginning the boiling process. Her eyelashes stood at attention as she glared back at him. He looked back and screamed, "Perez , where have you been with these troops"? "Not at the beauty parlor, I presume"! "You are a disgrace to the army, and you resemble a forty second street slut". "Take off those ridiculous eyelashes, this isn't broadway, this is the army" "You are going to conform to the rules, before they do the right thing, and kick your brown rear end out." Miss Perez just stood there a minute and then just dropped her pants, and gave him a full moon shot. She continued to stand there with her hands on her hips in a very challenging manner. She told him to kiss her behind and nothing else. The serjeant just shook his head in disgust, and he then, threw his hands up in the air. They somehow managed to get through the training that day. Mickey was later feeling so proud that she stood up to him. Carla called Robin at work from her duty station. She asked Robin to meet her at the service club in the old division.

When they met later that day, Carla and Robin were joined by the likes of a very robust, Mickey, who couldn't wait to tell them all about this morning. "Oh honey," she exclaimed, "you should have seen his face when I gave him the moon." "He wanted to kill me if he could. Carla and Robin laughed at this over a couple of colt fortyfives. They toasted her with a drink as being "the pride of Ft. Bragg". Mickey was all red and flushed, and replied, "You girls really think so"? They finished up their beers and headed for the bus stop. They couldn't keep those men waiting any longer at the house. The three of them were a sight at the bus stop, and more than one car stopped to get a better look. Robin was wearing a a sleeveless black top with a rhinestone studded lightening streak across the front. She had on white tight shorts, cut with a lot of provocation intended, very high. Carla was wearing a sheer almost see through nylon blouse over black silk stovepipe pants. She had her mascara and eyeliner on in such a way as to make her eyes slant upward. Her hair was even longer, with the auburn hairpiece she had added. Mickey was in a one piece number it was sleeveless and cut to hug the body. It was high on her brown legs which she had painted with leg paint. Her pumps were over three inches, and she had her hair up in a french twist. If you could call it that. It looked more like twisted frizz.

The bus arrived at the stop, just before there was a problem with their makeup melting away. The bus was loaded with eighty second airborne troops. They were all heading to town looking for some recreation. Carla felt someone pinch her and she let out a loud scream. Robin had a hand reach out and caress her breast area. Mickey had a hard slap on her can, before they made there way to a rear seat. Everyone turned around to gawk at the trio, but they paid them no mind. They were used to getting this much attention and so much more. A pair of guys came to where they were seated, and asked about their plans. The queens replied that they were going to the house, that they had rented and would they like to come along. Mickey was feeling left out because the two guys were talking to Carla and Robin. She began to remedy the situation by making spanish eves at a fellow across the aisle. She beckoned him to come and sit beside her and he did. Mickey told him he was so cute and asked him his name. He told her that it was Bill, and she repeated it to him seductively. He put her hand on his body and she squeeled approprietly. The other men were cheering when the queens and their new friends got off the bus. Mickey caught her heel on something and her friend had to keep her from falling. She squeeled her appreciation and they made ther way to the house. Waynetta greeted them at the door wearing an orange Tu Tu and long dangling earrings. She said that the truck drivers were all high and waiting for the party to begin. But not before Marty in Lorretta Young attire minus the box of tide.

Marty had on a Veronica Lake wig hanging of course over an eye. One eye was all this queen needed to scope out the scenery. Her earrings must have been at least a foot long and she had better be careful she didn't get one wrapped around her skinny neck. Her gown was flowing like a canapy and then some. She had the nerve to ask some man to pick up her train. Speaking of her behind it was wrapped tighter than a mummy's, before the material flared out to the floor. Everyone looked twice when they recovered their dropped jaws. She then proceeded to enter the room like the grand diva she thought she was. She of course demanded she be treated as such. Robin called upon Frauline Baker to do come in. She of course would have come in whether invited to do so or not. She wrappped her garment around one man and pulled him to her. He tried to protest but of course was rendered helpless. This happened to be the fourth of July and firecrackers were going off in the distance. Robin and Carla had two men to deal with and they started playing thir cards. The only breather they had so far was Marty's arrival. They of course were used to her theatrics. Robin had to put some music on and began to dance with one of the truckers. He took her full into his huge arms and began at once to kiss her neck and face with hot wet kisses. Carla and Waynetta joined her on the dance floor with their partners. Marty released her victim from her dress and he began to dance with her.She managed to get in her wiggles to the beat. One wondered how she could move in that tight fabric.

The two 82nd airborne troops were getting restless watching Carla and Robin dance with other men. Mickey had her trooper fixing her a drink and taking orders. Carla settled down between a ranger and a trucker and the airborne troop asked her if she was a leg. She replied that she was but that she was really flying tonight. She was especially high after that last double of 101 rum and coke. The coke didn't seem to water it down at all. He then told her he would like to have her along to go jumping with him. He asked her if she woul ever consider going to jump school. Just hen everyone jumped at the sound of a loud firecrakcer that someone had tossed into an open window. The thing hit on Marty's gown and tore through the fabric leaving a large black hole. She also had debris on and in her wig. The debris had imbedded itself in the strands and she took it off and began shaking it violently. It looked like a dish rag and everyone wondered where she had bought the thing. Well at least her makeup would be allright once she reapplied it. The sight of her bony head covered with a nylon stocking was too much. She had her temper up and decided to run down the culprit that tossed it through the window She could hardly walk in this gown let alone run. She fell on her powdered face after about two steps. She got up and took the entire gown off and stood there in her bloomers. She looked a sight with her gun powdered face,stocking cap, and baby blue bloomers tearing off down the street in pursuit.

She saw two teenage boys running and caught up to one in a zip. She lost her shoes somewhere between here and the house. She overpowered the boy and held him down on the grass. She had his bottom exposed and was giving him a sound spanking. She let him up when he said he was sorry. Soon the whole neighborhood was on the street watching. She realized what she must have looked like and headed back to the house in more of a hurry than when she left it. Mickey met her at the door and gave her a grasshopper and told her how proud she was of her chasing after the culprits, The others gave her a round of applause, which she gratefully accepted. Someone led her to the bathroom to clean up a little, but she seemed to enjoy her appearance. Carla just then made an appearance on the balcony with a new and wildly different outfit She seemed to be upset that Marty had been getting all of the attention. The gown she had on had a shimmering leopard effect. It was hanging over one shoulder and gathered oh so tightly at the waist. Her tiny boobs were pushed up on her favorite Frederick's push up bra. This gown had to have come from there also. She had on the longest earrings that hit on the railing when she bent over. Her makeup was highlighted in red tones from the Texas dust she she added to it. They used the powder in the theater and this girl was all theatrics when she beckoned to the people below. She gave them her very special sheba look. This look told them that she barely tolerated them. She cascaded down the stairs while everyone was thundersrruck.

Carla went over to a man and demanded he get her a drink. She took out a cigarette and motioned for someone else to light it. Robin and Mickey shared a laugh at the sight of Carla. The doorbell was ringing, Robin opened it to reveal a southern belle in the guise of Samantha. She had on her favorite beehive wig and lilac shiffon gown. This was topped off by a wide brimmed hat. She came in and in a rush of words told of her wild escape from her mother. It seemed her mother barged in to her room and caught her in this getup. She went on to say her mother tried to rid off her beehive wig and to add injury to insult bopped her up the side of the head. She said her mother screamed at her that she would never be no man's honey and to get that ridiculous outfit off. Samantha said that she hit her mother a few-times in the head with her handbag She then ran out of the house. She said that she got on a city bus to get here and that was another story. She said that her mother was going to call Marty's mother, and they knew.where the party was. Everyone let a loud yell out after they heard that. A man asked Marty how bad her mother was and she choked on her drink. Everyone prepared for the worst and they began to bolt the door. They locked all the windows and drew the drapes. The phone rang and everyone jumped up. Horn was on the line and he said he wanted to come over and bring Marcetto with him. Someone told him to come right over. Everyone started to get a little higher.

For the moment they forgot all about Marty's mother. Some one put on the song "Baby I need your loving", and they all began to dance. Mickey and Waynetta had stipped down to their bra and panties and were dancing up a storm. Mickey's bra was flaming red and had holes in it where her

78

nipples peeked out from the back part was backless and it looked like she had a string up her butt. Waynetta had on black satin high waisted panties with an over sized very stuffed bra. It must have belonged to her mother. Oh, if her mother saw her in these she would surely be in an altered state. The ranger's had had enough and soon stripped down and joined the pair on the dance floor. One of the men was grabbing Mickey and tossing her around like a jelly bean. He seemed to be severely aroused and it showed a lot by what he had on. Some one else threw Waynetta into the piano and began to make love to her on the keys, Carla looked at her and she looked back and just muttered somehow, "Oh child!!", Robin was teaching her partner how to dance and he was trying to undo her outfit. Carla was now being carried to a private area and he his privates didn't look so private. She had a look of cool amusement on her tiny face. The doorbell rang and everyone started to scatter, but it turned out to be Horn and Marcetto. They had with them two friends and wanted to be let in immediately.

Samantha let them in and introduced them to the floor show, and everyone on the sidelines. Marcetto heard the music and began immediately to dance alone. Someone picked the queen up and began to spin the child around. This only increased the mood that she was now enveloped in. The queen had all of her hair snipped off, and had big lips, that were painted a strange color. Everything about this person was strange. It looked like they were black and blue. The poor thing had gotten in the way of Mickey on the dance floor, and was whacked in the head, she came out of the situation still still spinning and she still had that dream like look on her face. A little while later someone was ringing the bell, but none-heard it ringing. A few moments later there was a loud crash on the door. Someone got up and opened it and was almost trampled by three irate women. The trio turned out to be, Marty's, Waynetta's, and Samantha' mothers. They had a look of pure fury in their eyes. Waynetta's mother took one look at her child in her very own underwear, and promptly fell out. While the other two women were busy desperately trying to revive her, people scattered in all directions. Marty came in from one of the bedrooms and stopped dead in her tracks. This came about after she had recognized her mother. When her mother in turn recognized her she began to call out her dead husband's name. She began to wail and moan how she had tried to bring up Marty in the proper manner. She looked at Marty again and lunged at her gown. She began to spin Marty around and began to unravel her extensive gown, Marty was so bombed that she could barely fight her off. Waynetta was trying to make a mad dash for the stairs, but her revived mother caught her by the panties. She was screaming out, "you quarr whore, Ill redden your behind". Waynetta turned around and began to tear at her mother's dress.

Waynetta was tearing her mother's dress so that she exposed a huge breast in the process. The two of them were halfway up the steps and began to roll down the stairs entangled with on another. Waynetta began to bite her mother's exposed breast. Her poor mother was screaming so loud, you couldn't hear the music. Samantha's mother was searching the place for her child. She found Carla, who was hiding in the bathroom. She pulled the cigarette out of Carla's mouth and began to question her. She called her every racial slurr she could muster up. Carla reacted in her usual disinterested way. She very cooly brushed past the woman. She gave her one of her one of her best, I can't even be bothered look Samantha appeared in the hall way and saw her mother and screamed. Her gown was flaring out, with its huge hoop skirt underneath. Her mother's nostrils flared out almost as much when she saw her in this get up. Samantha caught her heel in the rug and went flying down the stairs, beehive , hoop skirt, gown and all. She was blacked out at the bottom of the stairs in the ruins of her outfit. Her mother rushed to attend to her, wailing, "Oh Sam , what have I done to my baby". Please she said, "say something". Samantha came to and merely said, "Oh maw". Just then the police came to the door, and wanted to know what was going on. one of the neighbors had called complaining of the noise. Marty broke away from her mother and confronted the police, and tried to explain to them that it was just a costume party, and she had half of hers in shredds. Everyone began to leave after the police did. The three mothers were shown to the door by someone, but not after a lot of verbal thrashing by them as they were escorted out.

Waynetta's mother was trying to hold the top part of her dress together, the trucker's rode Robin and Carla back to the base. Carla was sitting very close to the driver, and acting very possessive. They were dropped off at the old division beer lounge. The queens found a seat next to Sylvester and Vallucci. Vallucci spotted Carla and pulled her to him calling her his little Gigi. Slylvester kissed Robin passionately. Fleming and Phil came in and came right over. They wanted to know immediately, how the party was over at the house. It seems the word had gotten out through Tina , who had heard that Mickey had attended. Carla gave them a bored look and said to them that it was the usual. The guys asked the girls if they would like to take a walk. They said of course they would. Fleming and Phil looked at each other knowingly as they walked out the door. The four of them walked to the back area of the service club, under the moonlit night. You could see a full moon through the tall pines. Robin held her head high and breathed in the sweet smell of magnolia and pine. She knew it would soon be even sweeter in Sylvester's arms. She dread the day her enlistment would be up, and she knew that it was soon to take place. Even if she did reup they would most likely send her someshere else. Carla had just a few more months on her's and she didn't want to go away either. Valucci asked Carla where she would go after her hitch. She replied that it would probably be to California. He told her that he would miss her, and then he smothered any further reply from her with his heavy kiss. Sylvester asked Robin if she would think of him when she was gone from here. Robin wiped a tear as she sang along with the radio.

The song was ," Dream a little dream of me". She sang it to his face and he was overcome by tenderness towards her. He thought that he would love to have Robin here for the remainder of his enlistment. He took her again into his arms and held her close. She put her hand inside his shirt and massaged his muscled chest. It was starting to get late and Robin had to head for her own area. It was a two mile walk under the stars. Sylvester decided to walk her there. Carla broke free from Vallucci and walked to her own area. She hadn't gotten far when she felt someone grab her from behind and put a hand over her mouth. The man told her that he had been wanting her and that this time he was taking what he wanted. He forced her to the ground and she of course pleaded for him to stop. He said yes to her no's and slipped her tight pants down around her ankles. She had gotten a dreamlike look on her face as she watched him

82

continue. He took her for all it was worth and they had gotten into a wild rythum. He then kissed her all the way up to her waiting mouth. After many more hot kisses they lay on their backs and looked up at the stars. They exchanged names and he explained that he had seen her from time to time. She told him she found his approach exciting if not unconventional. At that they both laughed and went on their separate ways. He managed to tell her that they would meet again. Robin and Sylvester reached her area, and exchanged kisses, and said their goodnights. Sylvester walked the long way back to his barracks. Robin used her flashlight to open up her combination lock on her locker. She stripped down to her bikini underwear, and caught Spade looking at her from his bunk. She returned his look and thought that he would soon make a move on her. She then layed on her bunk and put on her radio very low.

Robin began daydreaming at night and soon felt Spade's well muscled arm on her shoulder. She turned her head to find him gazing lovingly down at her. She returned a look of pure love and he climbed in beside her. He said nothing as he took her head from behind and brought his hungry lips down on hers. She was filled with passion for him and she realized that he felt the same for her. At that moment the others couldn't compare to him. He began to undress her and she helped him with his own garment. He fell on her and they realized a wild fury as they came together as one. She caressed his biceps and he in turn sqeezed her tender nipples. He then kised them with his his mouth and she found herself building up to a climax. He rode her to his own of equal height. They both collapsed on the bed truly exhausted and spent. You might say that they were well spent. Spade whispered to her that he found her beautiiful and exciting. She said that she often thought of him in the same terms. He kissed her softly one more time before retiring to his own bunk. Robin lay there for a while with the moon shining through the window. She wondered if it would ever be this wonderful again.

The morning brought the sounds of men rushing to get ready for duty. Robin was slow to rise and slow to get dressed. She hadn't wanted morning to come and melt away her night of pure bliss. She looked over at Spade and he felt her gaze and looked back lovingly. She then quickly got into her uniform and headed for the mess hall and breakfast.

At breakfast Spade sat next to her and held her hand under the table. She dreaded going to work, as much fun as she had there. She wanted to be with Spade. At the office she was preoccupied and couldn't seem to get on with her typing. Rick came in with his troops to be processed. Robin asked what he'd been up to, and this and that. Robin knew that this queen would leave no stone unturned, especially in the romance department. Rick said that he had been spending time with Tom. Rick said that Tom would be leaving for a base in Missouri, for basic training. Rick made plans to visit with him there when his tenure of duty was over here. That would not be too long in the future. Rick asked Robin to go skating with him tonight. Robin agreed to go, and they talked of little time they had at Bragg. Rick couldn't wait to get back to California and all that he had left behind. Later that evening Rick came over to Robin's barracks to meet Robin and spotted Demorest. She almost jumped out of her cut offs at the sight of him. Demorest was in the mirror combing his long hair. Rick immediately threw her arms around him and squealed. He was in shock as she threw her arms around him and massged his pectoral muscles. He had gotten some hairspray in his eye and wasn't too happy that this crazy queen was throwing herself all over him. He jumped away from her and felt like kicking her in her bubble butt. She was still squealing and didn't notice any apprehension on his part. She was still babbling on when Robin came to the rescue and asked him if he was allright. He gave Robin a look of pure gratitude in return.

Some of the other men in the barracks had taken notice of Rick and and his antics and were talking. They were treating Demorest a bit different as a result of this. Robin helped Demorest get the spray out of his eyes. He felt very tender toward her as she fussed over him. He wondered why she wasted her time with this exhibitionist. Rick was of course oblivious to all except what she wanted and she knew she wanted Demorest. Rick finally let Demorest alone and she and Robin headed for the main post area to catch a bus to town. Robin caught sight of Horn sitting up front very close to the driver They exchanged hellos and Robin noticed that he was pretty high from the bottle of Southern Comfort that he had on him. Horn of course inquired about Yale, whom she refused to stop chasing. Yale spent most of his time with a queen named Lacy. Lacy was set to leave any day now. Horn knew this and wanted to move on him. The bus headed for Hay street and the two queens headed for May's resturant and a little snack there. May was in there talking to Phil and Fleming and of course telling them the latest on her tempestous relationship with her infamous husband. Today he had taken all of her money from her purse and was out somewhere. May wanted them to check at his favorite bar to peek in on him. She wanted to be sure he wasn't keeping company with another woman . Robin and Rick had a coke float and a hamburger and headed out the door. They told Phil and Fleming they were going to the USO skating rink. They promised to meet them there later. Robin and Rick got a short distance and spotted a disturbance.

An irrate GI was hitting Carla, and she was spun around in a tizzy. It seems that she had refused to go with him to get a room at the Prince Charles hotel. She couldn't even be bothered when he asked her to pay for everything. Robin and Rick rushered over to her. She was screaming and her top was off and you could see her tiny little breasts with their brown nipples. Her leopard pants were torn and she was swinging her gold handbag at the fellow. Robin and Rick swept her away from the scene, but not before being groppled by more than one guy. The police were on their way and the queens hurried out of there. Carla had to make do with torn garments. Robin suggested that they go shopping and get some new garments. They went into the Belks store and looked around. The clerk was stammering and stuttering to the demands of Carla. She was trying on everything in sight. She finally settled on this black lace mini dress and paid for it. Robin and Rick found some other things and they soon headed out to the USO. When they arrived they found Phil and Fleming in the snack bar and told them of the latest adventure. Fleming said that it was very typical of them to get involved in something like that. Carla of course couldn't imagine what they were referring to. She cooly arranged her dress and pulled out a cigarette and waited for someone to light it. One guy who had witnessed the fracas, came over to Robin and asked her to skate with him. Robin thought, oh what the hell!! Robin gave it her best Dorothy Hamill, and Carla got up and did her Diahan Carroll. Carla was skating backwards and ran into some guy and bounced off him and ended up in the mens room. She fell on top of a toilet and nearly fell in. Fleming pulled the poor child out of the rest room. She had quite a day allready.

Someone suggested that they all go over to the red room and they all thought that that was a good idea and so they did. They found Wayenetta and Samantha sitting at one of the tables. The queens joined them and began to chatter. Waynetta reported having seen Babs earlier having a terrific fight with her boyfriend. Babs was running her big behind down Bragg blvd. When he caught up to the big heifer he whacked her so hard she spun into the traffic. She bounced off some slow moving car and landed on her feet. She ran after her friend like a huge, out of control, Rhino. They were fighting over something he wanted her to buy him. Waynetta and Samantha witnissed the spectacle while walking from Marty Baker's place. Robin asked how Marty was, and Waynetta said that Marty and her mother had another fight. Mary's mother caught Marty in bed with her boyfriend. Marty's mother walked in the bedroom. Marty was in such a state of sexual frenzy that she was light years away from her mother's voice. Marty's mother pulled her boyfriend from Marty and screamed at the two of them. Marty screamed for her to get out immediately. Waynetta was entering the house as Marty's mother was being shoved out. Marty then invited Samantha and Waynetta to come in. She told them all about the event. She confided in them like they were counselors. The queens at the red room ordered a pitcher of beer. Robin got up to use the rest room and some man put a hand on her arm and asked her to dance. She later joined him at his table. He said that he was a lieutenant in the green berets. They began to dance and he smelled her perfume and held her closely. He mentioned that he had a room upstairs and would she like to join him there. Robin agreed to do so and he smiled. Robin caught the sight of Marty entering the place, with her was he mother's so called boyfriend. She had her famous white turtle neck sweater on with a pair of the tightest red leather jeans. She just sizzled as she led her friend to the dance floor. The song on the jukebox was "Working in a coal mine", and this cow was working real hard on her mother's lover. She had no understanding of property rights. Her mother's boyfriend , as far as she was concerned was up for grabs. Babs and her boyfriend entered the bar and acted like nothing had happened. Babs kissed a stunned Waynetta as she sat her big behind down. Fleming asked Babs if she had been to the Dragon club and she replied that she had been in earlier. She said that it was crowded and full of men. Fleminng and Phil decided to go check out the club. Carla asked Marty's friend to dance and she began a slow grind with him. Carla couldn't have cared less what Marty or anyone else thought. Carla continued her shameless dance and Marty was visibly upset. Just then Marty looked up and saw her wildeyed mother enter the place. She was screaming out Marty's name and wanted to know wher her man was. She went over to Marty and grabbed her scarf and wrapped it around Marty's neck, nearly strangling the poor thing. She then spotted her beau dancing with Carla. She mentioned something of a racial nature and Carla merely looked very amused at her. Marty's mother grabbed her man and stormed out of the place. Carla quickly found herself a replacement and went on dancing.

Carla's new partner was a green beret and quite a hunk at that. He cupped his big hands around her beckoning behind and she moved on to the beat. Carla ground out a rythum with a sense of urgent abandonment. Babs and her beau began to dance and they were joined by Waynetta and

Samantha and two men they managed to drag onto the dance floor. After a few more dance numbers they made their way up to some of the rooms. Carla and Robin were being entertained by two men, who happened to have a two room suite. The group all made themselves comfortable and ordered room service. They had a bottle of champagne and some snacks sent up. Meanwhile in another room Marty was still fuming about her mother's activities when someone asked her about her heritage. She seemed to light up instantly and recanted to anyone who would listen about her Von Baker lines. She went into detail about the family crest and not to leave out the castle. Carla was soon two shades shy of naked with her partner. Robin of course was in the other room just talking with her friend. Carla and her man began rolling on the floor and it began to look like a log jam. Marty came into the room later and saw Carla and told her she should be ashamed of herself. Carla merely motioned for her to light her cigarette. She was on her tummy and was being taken for a ride. She had no sense of shame as she began smoking. Samantha was in a closet with her partner, she didn't care how small the thing was. Babs and her friend came in and Marty and the rest of the group were engrossed in conversation. Marty went over to the window and saw a catwalk. She wondered how it would be to venture out and experience the height. Marty went out on the ledge and was frozen with fear after walking a short distance. Babs looked out and heard her screams. Marty was in a precarious position to say the least.

Babs had her boyfriend go out and fetch the poor child back in. When Marty got back in she had someone get her a double. There was a knock on the door, and someone let in Rosemary and Tina, Rosemary looked very sexy in a mini dress. She began to talk of her plans to leave the army and run off to Germany with her officer boyfriend. Everyone was just shocked that she would tell the army her story and then leave. They all thought she was having too much fun here to leave. Tina wanted to know where the brazen Carla was. She knew she had to be tangled up with some man. She went into the next room and confirmed her suspicions. Carla said hi from her position on the floor and told Tina how wonderful it was. She then had Tina light her cigarette. She asked Carla if she had seen the notorious Mickey. Carla replied that she hadn't seen miss Perez. After a few more hours of this madness everyone left for the base. Robin got to her barracks about three oclock. She found Yale towelling down in the latrine. She said hello and he responded by coming over to her and letting his towel drop. He grabbed Robin and gave her hot kisses and much more. He then lead her to an empty barracks next door. They began making an urgent love. After he had finished she tried to make up her mind whom she preferred. Was it Spade, Sylvester. She liked all three so very much that she couldn't make up her mind. They lay back on the bunk and Robin caressed Yale's broad chest. He fondled her breasts and rubbed her silky legs. He told her that once was not enough and she agreed. Robin lay in Yale's strong arms until the first light of dawn. They then headed back to get ready for duty.

Carla was at her own unit getting prepared for three days in the field. They were a combat unit and even though Carla was an admin clerk in her M.O.S., the child had to be combat ready with the rest of the unit. Carla began to dust her steel pot and get all the cobwebs out of her gear. Lern was looking on as Carla busied herself getting ready. His mind was on other things as he watched Carla. He got especially turned on as she reached for something high in her locker. He had full plans for her in the next three days. Everyone was ready to go and they loaded up everything including themselves in this huge ten wheeler truck. Lern managed to sit next to Carla and he wasted no time. When they arrived at the camping site, Carla and Lern were engaged in setting up their tent. The tent was capable of housing two people. Lern couldn't wait until it was time for them to turn in. After this they headed over to the mess tent. Lern followed after Carla like she was a bitch in heat. Carla finished her tray of food and took out a cigarette, expecting of course for someone to instantly light it. As she took a long draw on her cigarette, she said that she could not possibly imagine how they expected her to be combat ready. She could barley get enough energy to pull a trigger. They had a five mile hike after dinner and Carla was dreading it. She thought to herself that she couldn't even be bothered with this madness. She wondered how she ever got into a combat unit. The hike was moving along with Carla dragging herself and Lern behind her lending some support. Carla managed to step into a hole letting out a huge scream. Lern rescued her and tenderly helped her to her feet. After more of this, they made their way back.

Carla got into her sleeping bag and Lern muscled his way right next to her. He instantly wanted oral gratification and he took the initiative in getting her started. She was shocked to say the least. They managed to do a few more things before dawn. At dawn they had breakfast and had to assemble and reassemble their M sixteen rifles. Carla knew absolutely nothing about this. She had Lern do her's for her. They next had to run in and out of fox holes covering the man in front. Carla couldn't even get out of the first foxhole and when she did she almost shot the man she was supposed to be covering. This was so hard on her nails and she needed to rub in some skin cream. Being out in the open was horrible on her skin. They were on the range firing at targets. Carla managed to hit a few in the next lane. At the obstacle course she had managed to become an obstacle, for heaven's sake. On the overhead bars they were supposed to navigate, she fell in the mud on the second bar. She blacked out and had to be revived with a cold towel. That night she lay exhausted in Lern's arms. She was glad it was almost over, she couldn't take much more. The next day they had a search and destroy mission and they were in camouflage uniforms. They were in small squads operating in the thick forest. Carla lost her way somehow and was separated from her squad. They finally located her after she screamed herself nearly hoarse. She was so glad when it was time to go back to the base and end all of this foolishness. Lern sat next to her in the truck and he put her hand where he wanted it. As the truck rolled in the old division, Micky was standing ther waiting. She spotted Carla and let out a huge scream. Carla screamed back at her and told her to wait for her in the service club.

As Carla unpacked her duffle bag her bunkmates asked if the queen had remembered to pack her leg cream. Carla quickly produced several tubes from her duffel to show she hadn't forgotten. She had one man look into her bag at her seven day collection. She noticed that this talk was making him aroused. She put her hand where she shouldn't have and he let out a moan. He then pushed her behind some lockers and took her wildly. She let out a few of her own brand of moans. Carla then dragged her tired buns to the showers. Later she met Mickey at the service club. Mickey had just been shopping and wanted to show her the latest additions to her makeup collection. She let Carla try on some false eyelashes. They looked at least an inch long. She also mantioned that Marty was having another get together at her place. When they arrived at miss Bakers, she was in the kitchen preparing some snacks. She was wearing a mini apron over her mini dress. She of course had her hair in a respectable bun. Under her dress she revealed to all her Frederick's cut out panties. The cut outs were over her buns and they lifted and made them jut out somewhat. She knew she was provacative and that she could provoke almost anything or anyone. She screamed for a solid minute when she saw Mickey and what she had on. Robin and Horn entered through the front door. Robin rushed over and asked Carla about her training session in the field. Carla said she would tell everyone later. Rosemary and Lieutenant arrived along with Tina and Babs. Everyone asked Rosemary about her discharge and if she had told them her story. She said that she had done today and she and her friend were leaving for Germany at the end of the week.

Everyone hugged her and said they would surely miss her and all the good times they shared here. Phil and Fleming arrived a second later. They rushed in and told everone how these troops had harrassed them. They were on the bus and someone had noticed Phil's hairpiece and pulled it off. He was trying desperately to retrieve it and they threw him around the bus. Fleming was helpless to do anything. They called him a chocolate queen. They had soaked his piece with beer by the time he got it back. He asked Marty if he could wash and dry the thing in his bathroom. Lucky for him he had a baseball cap to put on while he waited for it to dry out. Waynetta and Samantha arrived and twirled around in their new outfits. Waynetta was wearing a two piece matching vest and very large ballooning pantaloons. She had on a white ruffled blouse and completed the picture with spiked heels. Samantha had on skin tight levis with a white fluffy angora sweater and huge block heels. Carla had on a long leather coat which she took off to reveal a leopard jumpsuit with big top leather boots. They were high button style to her liking. She looked as if she were trying to pull an Elsa Martinelli number on everyone. Marty entered the room with a huge tray of goodies for everyone to enjoy. She had her favorite bartender miss Mickey Perez set up to fix drinks. Marty began telling anyone who would listen about her adventure last night at the Prince Charles hotel. It seems she had met this number at the Red Room lounge and proceeded with him up the stair case, when they were abruptly stopped by the desk clerk. No guest was permitted in the room after ten. She was shocked by her friend when he suggested she climb the fire escape to his room. He looked out the window while taking Marty up the rickety staircase that served as a fire escape. This hotel was to be torn down and it didn't have much life in it. Marty managed to climb two flights and had two more to go. She wondered if the this thing would hold up under her weight. The landing almost gave way on the very next flight up and when she stepped up off it the thing almost tore away from the building. She saw her friend at the window urging her on. When she finally fell into his room she was thoroughly exhausted. Afterwards they made love and she thought that it was well worth the climb. She felt so good she called her mother and cussed her out thoroughly. Waynetta looked out the window and saw a busload of football players. She ran out and flagged the bus down. The next thing you knew they were in the house and ready to party down. When Marty saw them coming in she jumped up and let out her Jane yell, very much like Tarzan's. The jocks were beginning to seek out romantic partners. The girls were just squealing with delight at this intrusion. Some on put on some music and couples began to make their way to the dance floor. Carla was lifted up by some hunk and made to dance which she did immediately. Robin was escorted by some blonde hulk. Marty was on the shoulders of someone. Mickey was floored by another and was just sqealing with pure delight. Babs was in heat with some stranger, where was her boyfriend? She wasn't too concerned with his whereabouts. Waynetta was being tossed about like a pick up stick by someone else. He didn't know a thing about dancing. She didn't seem to mind. Carla was being man handled by her partner and she slapped him. He told her that was no way to act, and she merely threw her head back and laughed.

Carla decided that she had enough of this and asked Robin if she was ready to leave. They made their way to Bragg Blvd. and a bus back to the fort. The bus they got on of course was loaded with airborne troops. The girls went to find a seat in the back of the bus. Someone was rubbing Robin's back and she turned around to see the cute man who was doing it. She let him continue and pretended to be interested in what Carla had to say. Carla was rambling on about her upcoming discharge and going to Calif. Robin was busy the next day making the transition from the record processing section to the orderly room. This wasn't going to be fun working with this gung ho major that was in charge. He was strictly military and wanted no fun and games. There were some civilian women working here. One was a tall fortyish number who was obsessed with her own glamour. She said something bout the time being near for her facelift. There also was a plump queen, named Joeton who belonged to a clique of closet gays. She was almost civil to Robin. Hernandez also worked in the orderly room He was all worked up to have Robin so close to him.

He had an erection nearly all day and he couldn't resist not following Robin into the latrine. He found her combing her blue black hair out. He slowly approached her and said that he knew that Robin had always wanted to kiss him. She merely looked at him through the mirror and said, as a matter of fact , that it was the other way around. Robin got up to leave and tried to get by him, but he grabbed her and kissed her savagely. She thought she would let him get it out of his system. He had an enormous erection and put Robin's hand on it. He wouldn't let her take it away. He put his tongue deep into Robin's mouth and stated to grind against her. He did this for a while. She knew that someone was bound to walk in at any moment. She told him to stop and promised to meet him later. She said they could meet in the day room. He gave her one last kiss, and let her go. She straightened her uniform up and walked demurely back to her desk. Hernandez came out of the latrine with not the coolest of expressions on his face and his member was at a ninety degree angle in his pants. He was visibly flushed as he tried to hide his aroused state. Robin thought that he was a bit out of control. That night she did go to the day room, just out of curiosity, to see how far he would go. When he showed up he wasted little time after locking the door. He took off his shirt and revealed a hairy well muscled chest for Robin to admire. He was very aroused and Robin couldn't help but notice. He took his trousers off in a jiffy and began to help Robin out of her cutoffs. She wasn't sure if she should go through with this. He was enormous by normal standards and it might be painfull. He playfully teased her nipples and had her pressed up aginst the wall. He rubbed his hands up and down the length of her body marveling at her silky skin. She began to lose control of the situation as he proceeded to have her. just as he was bout to enter her body she managed

96

to brake free. She bolted for the door and ran down the stairs to her barracks. He was furious to say the least. Robin later had Carla over to run into town with. Robin wanted to know how long it would be before they had some new barracks. A queen couldn't even dress in privacy. Carla sympathized with her. She said that the man knew every shade of panties she had.

They sometimes broke into her locker, to see them, and hang them out for others to also. Robin suggested that they go over to the snack bar nearby. The juke box blared out "Love is here and now your gone". Robin and Carla sipped on some Colt forty fives, and settled down to some gossip. It seems that Mickey was in trouble again for groping some recruit in her unit. Robin wasn't too surprised at the antics of the notorious Miss Perez. Hernandez and Cedeno came into the snack bar and sat next to the girls. Cedeno pinched Carla on the backside and Hernandez put his arm around Robin very tenderly. They asked the girls to go with them to the service club. They decided to go with them and walked to the main post area, which wasn't too far. They had to walk through a secluded area and the boys wasted no time in taking full advantage of the situation. The boys planted kisses on the girls and picked them up and carried them for a while. Robin's little radio played the song , "Ninety Six Tears". When they arrived the girls had to apply fresh makeup. Carla and Robin went to the ladies room to apply fresh makeup and the boys ordered their drinks. Carla asked Robin why she had never mentioned these two. Robin replied that she had never given them much thought. She then told Carla that they were always fighting to get behind them in the mess line. Carla said that she and her crowd would have serviced them right away. They slow danced with the boys to a Chris Montez number.

Hernandez held Robin very close and whispered love words in her ear.

Robin after hearing Hernandez and his tokens of love, just had an amazed look on her face. After Cedeno squeezed the life out of Carla, they sat down. Horn walked in with his bus driver friend. They sat very close together in a booth and were obviosly very high. They weren't concerned with other people and what they were thinking. Horn spotted Robin out of the corner of her eye and rushed over to greet her. She had her friendliest smile on to greet the two of them. Horn immediately wasted no time in revealing that Marty was having another of her famous parties. Everyone lit up and decided to ride in the bus with Horn and the driver. When they arrived at Marty's they came to screeching halt and nearly knocked down the front door. The music inside was very loud and could be heard halfway down the block. Carla knocked on the front door and Marty answered with her famous Jane yell. She greeted the girls with slaps on their behinds and the boys with seductive smiles. Waynetta and Samantha were seated in the living room and Mickey was of course mixing drinks. Marty was telling Waynetta that that cow Babs was arriving later with Archibald and Agram. These were black friends of Carla and Mickey who were from Puerto Rico. Waynetta's serjeant friend opened the door and rushed to her skinny arms. Marty got up to dance and she had on a frog green sarong. Soon everyone got into the act and the floor was crowded with a melting pot of people. Carla then sprayed Channel around the room. Mickey was doing the bird with a drink in one hand. Carla almost split her leather pants as she bent this way and that. Horn and his bus driver were lost in a drunken kiss. Waynetta and her serjeant were doing a tango of some sort and he threw her through the revolving doors into kitchen.

Marcetto just happened to be in the kitchen in a dreamlike trance as if she were listening to Streisand. Another group of people arrived from the Stein room. Robin recognized a serjeant from her unit. He liked to wear his uniform out. Marty jumped on his shoulders as she greeted him. He said hello to Robin whom he recognized from his unit. Marty's mother phoned and wanted to know what the hell was going on there. She said that she just might decide to come over to inspect. Marty threw the phone down and put on the record, Cool Jerk, and almost jerked her skinny form into a pretzel. She grabbed Marcetto out of his preoccupation, onto the dance floor. Marty said that the liquor was about to run out and wanted to know who would fetch some. Hernandez decilded to go in Marty's car. He asked Robin to ride with him. Waynetta and her beau wanted to ride along. The car was a hot sixty seven camaro. Hernandez wasted no time in reving up the engine. Waynetta and her friend were locked in an intertwining embrace and were being jostled about the back seat. Finally she broke free and told Hernandez to slow down. They were being followed by the police and Hernandez decided to lose them. They lost the patrol car and headed into the trailer of Jim, he was a friend of Waynetta. He invited them in and they settled down to a drink and conversation while they waited for some time to pass. They headed back to Martys after picking up some liquor. When they returned Marty was so glad to see them, she let out her Jane yell.

After a few moments there was a knock on the door. Marty answered it and revealed her infamous mother. She looked as if she had been drinking. She immediately yelled at Marty about the party. Marty hit her as hard as she could up the side of her southern head. She hit Marty back, and they were soon entwined all over the floor. After a while they both fell back in a dead faint. Everyone resumed dancing as if nothing went on. She had come here one time and threw all of Marty's drag outfits out the window, and Marty hit her so hard she was knocked out. When she awoke she knocked Marty through a window and she was hanging out the window with a boa for a choker. Marty got up from the sofa where she fell and told everyone not to mind her mother. She said that she would throw her out when she woke up. Robin and Carla decided to head back to the base. When Robin arrived she came upon Spade in her baracks. He was preparing for his workout and was arranging his weights. As he worked out Robin took notice of his bulging muscles. He was aware of her prescence and glanced over at her on occasion. He continued with his workout until it was through and then he went into the latrine for his shower. When he came back out he caught Robin's eye and smiled. He st at the edge of her bunk and Robin almost lost her breath when he rubbed her leg. He then touched her lips and bent down and kissed them. She marveled at the urgency of his mouth and was engulfed by him. She felt his manly chest as he pulled her so close to him. He then lay down on top of her and said that he wanted to know all of her beauty. They lay together for the rest of the evening. Carla saw Vallucci at the service club and he told her he was leaving at the end of the month. He took her hand and said that he would surely miss her. She formed tiny tears around her tiny eyes and thought of all the good times they had. What she wondered could top this. Robin arrived with Yale and they all danced to the song, "Cherish". They danced as if they would not be seeing much of each other after this. On the day of Vallucci's departure Carla was at work typing in a daze. She actually got more done today than usual. When her day of duty was over she met him at the day room. He told her he wouldn't ever forget her as she let out little sobs. He then kissed her and called her his little Gigi one last time. Carla saw him to his bus and nearly ran after it as it pulled out. Vallucci waved from the bus. Later she decided to go out with Robin. They went to Belks department store and found Marty trying on some high heels. The sales lady was a nervous wreck with Marty trying on everything. She had on one pair, that the sales girl said, were not for her. Marty replied that she was a show girl and these would do nicely. Later Robin and Carla went to the skating rink and began to reminice about all the times that they spent here. Robin talked of Rick and how much he liked to skate. It hadn't been too long that he had left. Carla brought up Vallucci again and started to get misty. She told Robin it might be a good idea to find some beaus tonight to help them forget.

ABOUT THE AUTHOR

Robin Natrigo is a singer, songwriter and actor who has recorded a few songs and has published a few poems. Natrigo has had stage and film roles and has sung in a few clubs. Los Angeles's best kept secret is Robin Natrigo. The man behind Glenn Frey's hit "The Heat is On" is a veritable music machine. He has well over 200 songs to his credit, has appeared with both the L.A. City College Choir and the Southeast Theatre Conference, and has played his own songs in numerous nightclubs as well as showcases by Lone Hill Records and Hollywood Artists Records. Eclectic and entertaining, his style recalls that of another Robin: Robyn Hitchcock. Danceable, singable, and likable, Natrigo's pop gems are impossible to resist.